HAPPINESS
BECOMES YOU

ALSO BY TINA TURNER

My Love Story

I, Tina

HAPPINESS
BECOMES YOU

A GUIDE TO
CHANGING YOUR LIFE
FOR GOOD

TINA TURNER

WITH TARO GOLD AND REGULA CURTI

ATRIA BOOKS

NEW YORK   LONDON   TORONTO   SYDNEY   NEW DELHI

ATRIA
BOOKS

An Imprint of Simon & Schuster, Inc.
1230 Avenue of the Americas
New York, NY 10020

First Atria Books hardcover edition December 2020

ATRIA B O O K S and colophon are trademarks of Simon & Schuster, Inc.

For information about special discounts for bulk
purchases, please contact Simon & Schuster Special Sales at
1-866-506-1949 or business@simonandschuster.com.

The Simon & Schuster Speakers Bureau can bring authors to your live event. For
more information or to book an event, contact the Simon & Schuster Speakers
Bureau at 1-866-248-3049 or visit our website at www.simonspeakers.com.

Interior design by Kyoko Watanabe

Manufactured in the United States of America

1 3 5 7 9 10 8 6 4 2

Library of Congress Cataloging-in-Publication Data is available.

ISBN 978-1-9821-5215-4
ISBN 978-1-9821-5217-8 (ebook)

I dedicate this book to you . . .
in honor of your
unseen efforts to
triumph over each problem
life sends your way.

Contents

INTRODUCTION

Wherever I go, I'm touched when people tell me how inspired they are by my life story, by the challenges I've overcome during my eight decades on this planet.

I'm a survivor by nature, but I've had help, and I don't mean success, or money, although I've been blessed with both. The help that has been essential to my well-being, my joy, and my resilience is my spiritual life.

That's a big statement, easy to say, harder to explain. But here, in *Happiness Becomes You: A Guide to Changing Your Life for Good,* it is my greatest pleasure to share with you the story of my spiritual journey.

I always wanted to be a teacher, but I believed I should wait for the moment when I had something important to say, when I was sure how to offer real wisdom.

That time is now.

As I write these words, we're in the midst of the worst pandemic of the last hundred years. From this tragedy, many of us have mourned the loss of loved ones, while many more have sadly lost their livelihoods. My heart aches as I stand with you in this new, uncertain landscape.

Even if you're among the rare few who avoided the direct impact of this calamity, we all know that no one gets through life without facing adversity. More than ever, I believe we must choose hope, and use our difficulties to move ourselves onward and upward.

I've reflected a lot about adversity over the past decade while I battled a series of severe health crises that nearly killed me. Through it all, I had many opportunities to review my life and ask myself some tough questions.

How did I overcome so many serious problems? You might know the list, and it's long—an unhappy childhood, abandonment, an abusive marriage, a stalled career, financial ruin, the premature death of family members, and multiple illnesses.

There were so many external circumstances and forces I couldn't change or control, but my life-altering revelation was that I could change my way of responding to these challenges. The most valuable help comes from within, and peace comes when individuals work on becoming their better selves. I started that work in my thirties, when I discovered the transformative power of spirituality.

Spirituality isn't tied to any one religion or philosophy. It isn't the property of a priesthood or clergy. Spirituality is a personal awakening and relationship with our Mother Earth and the universe that increases openness and positivity.

My awakening began five decades ago through my practice and study of Buddhist teachings. Sharing the story of this most precious part of my life with you is a long-cherished dream. This book carries my personal guidance on how to create lasting happiness. It explains spiritual truths I've learned on my unlikely path to joy, from childhood to today.

Here, I reveal my greatest untold life lessons, deepest realizations, and beloved ancient principles to help you recharge your soul.

I offer you these insights so you'll have the tools to overcome your own obstacles—even if your challenges seem as impossible as those I've faced—and achieve your own dreams, so that you may become truly happy. I want you to open up your heart and mind, refresh your spirit with new hope, courage, and compassion, and change the world by changing your life.

Let me show you all the wonderful ways that *Happiness Becomes You.*

TINA TURNER
May 3, 2020

Chapter One

NATURE'S WELCOME

Thank you for being you, exactly as you are. Thank you for the tapestry of your life experiences, which have led you to read these words I've written just for you.

Thank you for opening this book, so I may share with you the spiritual lessons I've learned through more than eighty years of living.

Each of us is born, I believe, with a unique mission, a purpose in life that only we can fulfill. We are linked by a shared responsibility: to help our human family grow kinder and happier.

I first learned about the workings of the universe from my daily experiences growing up in Nutbush, Tennessee, a small rural town. I loved spending time outside, running through the fields, looking up at the heavenly bodies in the sky, spending time with animals—domestic and wild ones—and listening to the sounds of nature.

Even as a little girl, I sensed an unseen universal force as I walked through the wide-open pastures each day. Communing with nature taught me to trust my intuition, which always seemed to know the way home when I was lost, the best branch on a tree for swinging, or where a treacherous rock was hidden in a stream.

I learned to listen to my heart, which taught me that you and I are connected to each other and everything else on this planet. We are joined together by the mysterious nature of life itself, the fundamental creative energy of the universe.

In this complicated world of ours, where contradictions abound, we find breathtaking beauty in the most unlikely places. The brightest rainbows appear after the heaviest of storm clouds. Magnificent butterflies emerge from the drabbest cocoons. And the most beautiful lotus flowers bloom from the deepest and thickest mud.

Why do you suppose life works this way?

Perhaps those rainbows, butterflies, and lotus flowers are meant to remind us that our world is a mystical work of art—a universal canvas upon which we all paint our stories, day by day, through the brushstrokes of our thoughts, words, and deeds.

Even though I've felt it instinctively since childhood, it wasn't until I was in my early thirties that I began to consciously see life in this way. I'm not sure if the nine-year-old me handpicking cotton in Tennessee specifically dreamed of a day when the forty-nine-year-old me would be shaking hands with the Queen of England. Yet, on some deep level, even that far-fetched dream was always within the field of my imagination.

Who would have expected any extraordinary outcome from a farm girl like me, born between the final days of the Great Depression and the first days of World War II? Nevertheless, my life's path has truly been like a lotus flower, blooming over and over again, against all odds, emerging stronger each time.

No matter where you're born or who your parents are, it seems to me that we all start out with a mixture of circumstances, with both darkness and light. Some of us experience more of one than the other. And I believe there is an inextricable link between us and our ancestors, that we stand on the shoulders of those who came before us.

If there's one lesson I've learned, it's that encountering adversity, as I have, isn't necessarily a bad thing. It's what we make of it, how we use it to shape ourselves and our futures, that ultimately determines our success and happiness.

The thicker the mud, the stronger the lotus that blooms from it, rising above the muck to reach the sun. The same is true for people. I know, because I did it. And I know you can, too.

How did I do it? That's what I want to tell you.

My hometown of Nutbush is nestled along the

honeysuckle-lined roads of West Tennessee's Haywood County. Haywood was and still is a quiet agricultural area with deep religious roots. It is home to Tennessee's oldest Jewish synagogue, built in 1882, as well as the places where members of my family have long worshipped, the Spring Hill Baptist Church and the Woodlawn Baptist Church, both founded by an emancipated slave named Hardin Smith. Secretly educated by a plantation owner's wife, Smith grew up to become a respected preacher and established the congregation that became the Woodlawn Baptist Church, where my grandfather and father later served as deacons.

Thanks to Reverend Smith's emphasis on education, by the turn of the twentieth century, our county had the highest literacy rate among the Black population of Tennessee. One of the schools Reverend Smith founded for Black children became Carver High School, which I attended. He also organized Black musicians and singers, providing opportunities for them to perform, and laid the foundation for the region's strong musical traditions, from which I later benefited.

I arrived at the end of 1939, safely delivered in a windowless basement relegated to "colored" women's maternity at the county hospital. My parents named me Anna Mae, the only name I was known by until adulthood.

My father, Richard Bullock, was the managing sharecropper for a white family called the Poindexters. We had our own four-room home and an acre-size garden filled with vegetables, next to the Poindexters' home and farm.

White folk rarely welcomed Black people to their homes, but my older sister, Alline, and I were often invited to enjoy lemonade and snacks with the Poindexters. It was only when they had other white people around that we knew we couldn't go in.

Racism was common, and like many southern counties during the mid-twentieth century, ours was not immune to violence. The year after I was born, Tennessee's last known lynching happened not far from our home.

A man named Elbert Williams was one of our area's first civil rights organizers. In 1940, Mr. Williams tried to register Black voters—a right that had long been denied. He soon paid the ultimate price for that brave act. One horrible night, he was abducted from his home by a sheriff and a gang of other white men who brutally ended his life.

Mr. Williams's murder silenced the civil rights movement in our county for two decades.

I sometimes saw that sheriff, still on duty despite his crimes. People didn't talk about it. Things like that simply weren't discussed. There was a fragile calm among the segregated citizens of Haywood County that no one wanted to disturb.

Although racism was rampant, I had more immediate things to worry about, starting with the early realization that my parents couldn't stand each other. They fought constantly, locked in a hopeless battle neither could win. Their unhappiness cast a long shadow over my childhood.

What an endless chain
of unhappiness
prejudice forges.
—LENA HORNE

•

"Love thy neighbor"
is a precept which could transform the world
if it were universally practiced.
—MARY McLEOD BETHUNE

My mother, Zelma, was affectionate with my sister, but it was different for me. I knew I was the child my mother never wanted. That's a heavy burden for a little girl to bear.

My parents tried to get away from Nutbush a number of times, hoping that a change of scenery would give them a new life, and they left their young daughters behind. When I was only three, they went to work at a military base in Knoxville, more than 350 miles away. We didn't have a phone, so we had no contact while they were gone. It would have felt closer if they had moved to the moon, since at least I could see the moon.

Though my mother was always emotionally distant from me, her side of the family was warm and caring. I adored my fun-loving grandmother, Mama Georgie, and my cousin Margaret, who was three years older than me. Margaret became my first mentor, best friend, and soul sister, and in some ways she was even a mother figure—including having "the talk" with me as I entered adolescence, the only person who did.

When my parents went away, they sent Alline to live with Mama Georgie and left me with the other side of our family, my paternal grandparents, Mama Roxanna and Papa Alex, who were strict and somber Bible-thumping folks. It was agony for me. I was high-spirited and playful. I loved to run in the fields, get down in the dirt, yell to my friends, dance through the house, let my hair fly free. Not one bit of my natural rambunctiousness was allowed in their house.

Mama Roxanna forced me to go to church, and my lack of enthusiasm was compounded by the sweltering heat inside the building. There was no air-conditioning, of course, and it was baffling to my young mind that everyone got all dressed up just to go sit in a hot oven and listen to someone lecture. I never understood what the preacher was talking about, since no one bothered to explain it to the children. For me, sitting there, drenched in sweat, it was just a tedious exercise in boredom.

At one point, my parents let us visit them in Knoxville. While we were there, we attended a Pentecostal church, which was a very different experience from our subdued Baptist church. The "sanctified" church could get wild and turned out to be much more enjoyable for me. People would sometimes "get the Spirit" and start yelling, dancing, and singing in the aisles. It was definitely action packed, which was more my style. I'd join right in, singing and dancing.

One day I got so carried away that I danced right out of my skirt. Some folks would even fall down and go into convulsions. I just figured they must have gotten too excited. Although the Pentecostal experience didn't resonate with me any more than the quieter Baptist services, it was a real spectacle. And it was fun!

Back home, Baptist Sunday school became obligatory. Sometimes it was pleasant because it was nice to be with other children. But when I finally got old enough to join the choir, that was my sweet spot. I was eight or nine, and the youngest singer in the group. The rest were teenagers. Even at that young age, I had the biggest voice in the choir and would often be chosen to sing a solo. Since we had no telephone at home, I had learned to broadcast my voice to friends and neighbors without hurting my vocal cords, which helped my voice grow strong, a talent that came in handy later in my life.

My parents returned to Nutbush when I was five, so I was freed from the stifling environment at my relatives' place. But our home wasn't much better because my parents were still fighting tooth and nail.

Whenever they'd go at each other, I'd run out of the house to find a quiet place to calm my heart. Sitting by a stream, I'd watch dragonflies hover over the water, swoop onto the surface to quench their thirst, then zoom off, disappearing as quickly as they had appeared.

I daydreamed about growing my own wings so I could fly off to a happier place—a home where nobody fought and I could be loved for being myself.

That was just a dream. When I was eleven, my mother left for the last time and never came back. She moved to St. Louis. Never sent a single letter. Nothing. I waited for the mail to come each day, hoping she would remember me, but I didn't see her again until Mama Georgie's funeral, more than five years later.

Soon after I turned thirteen, my father also left. His destination was Detroit.

Go within every day
and find the inner strength so that
the world won't blow your candle out.
—KATHERINE DUNHAM

•

Everyone has a gift for something,
even if it is the gift of being
a good friend.
—MARIAN ANDERSON

At first, my father made an effort to stay in touch, and he'd send a little money every now and then to help my relatives take care of me. But he never came back. I was a child with no parents and no real home.

Thankfully, I still had my cousin Margaret.

Margaret and I were each other's sounding board and safe haven, sharing our dreams and confiding our secrets. When I was fourteen, she told me a secret I never expected to hear: She was pregnant. This news confused me, because Margaret was always so careful in her life. She was only seventeen and didn't fool around with boys as much as some other girls did, and her biggest dream was to attend college.

She confided in me that she had decided a baby and college weren't compatible, so she was determined to terminate the pregnancy. She didn't know how, though, so she tried old-time home remedies, like drinking warm concoctions of black pepper, in vain attempts that only resulted in an upset stomach and a foul taste in her mouth.

Tragically, at the end of January 1954, just a week after she revealed her biggest secret to me, Margaret died in a terrible car accident.

I couldn't believe it. Not my Margaret. The light of my life. I was devastated. Lost. Alone.

Death was something I hadn't thought much about before Margaret's passing. I had gone to Papa Alex's funeral when I was eleven, but honestly, when I saw him lying still in the casket, he just looked like he was in a tranquil sleep.

Losing Margaret was very different. Nothing had ever struck me as hard.

I had witnessed the circle of life and death in nature, where plants and animals came and went in their own time. And I had heard about deaths in our community, young and old people, dying in all sorts of circumstances. But this time it was very personal.

After Margaret died, there was a lot of talk about God's will. Our community was deeply Baptist, after all, and that was a natural response to the sudden tragedy that killed her and a few other young people, including my half sister Evelyn (my mother's child from a previous relationship). Thinking about the mysteries of life and death, I didn't have a problem with the concept of an underlying universal force. But the idea of a bearded old white man in space, monitoring activities here on Earth, felt unrelatable and just plain unreal.

I couldn't verbalize my own vision of God then, as the vocabulary hadn't come to me yet. But from the youngest age I can recall, I knew I could experience "Godliness" in Mother Nature. Something told me I had a piece of God in my heart, even if the traditional beliefs of my family and the way they practiced religion weren't right for me. I wished they practiced what they preached and lived more positive lives.

After Margaret's death especially, I knew I'd have to find my own way to carry on, to construct my own path to happiness.

I spent a lot of time outside, where I could think in peace.

Nature was the only place where I always felt welcome and enjoyed a sense of belonging—my truest childhood home. Whether sitting in the garden at night staring up at a star-filled sky or lying in the noon shade of a tulip tree, watching butterflies glide by, I felt the healing force of love everywhere in nature, and I soaked it in.

I didn't let my unstable family situation prevent me from finding enjoyment in the world around me. In those days, Nutbush and other areas north of Memphis were a mecca for local and traveling gospel, blues, and jazz musicians. They performed in our churches, cafés, and juke joints and became my first musical influences. I loved listening to all different types of music, and I did so every chance I got. We didn't have a record player, but we always had a radio, and that was good enough for me.

I enjoyed singing in the church choir and occasionally performed with Mr. Bootsie Whitelow, a popular Nutbush native, and his String Band. During high school, my music teacher even had me learning to sing opera. I had other interests as well, and excelled at cheerleading, track, and basketball.

But most of all, I loved movies. Every chance I got, I'd go to our local movie theater, often memorizing scenes on the spot and reenacting them for my family when I got home. After I saw *Little Women,* I enjoyed acting out the scene where Jo and Amy (played by June Allyson and Elizabeth Taylor) pretend to faint. One time, I did such a convincing job of falling lifeless to the floor that my sister got scared, thinking I'd actually passed out!

Fantasies about the silver screen often got me through difficult times. When I was working in the fields, picking cotton and strawberries in the oppressive heat, I would imagine a far-off paradise where I could live like the elegant movie stars did. I had no idea where this magical "Hollywood" was, but I knew, deep down inside, that I wasn't destined to stay in the farmlands. Even then, I believed that my circumstances did not limit my possibilities. I knew that someday I'd find my way out into the world.

My summer visit to Knoxville at age five had already given me a taste of another world—one with towering brick buildings, broad streets, and sparkling clean stores filled with the latest products. Now, eleven years later, when Mama Georgie suddenly passed away, my mother invited me to live with her in St. Louis. That's when I began a whole new life.

Living in a big city for the first time, I felt like an outsider. Then again, I had always felt like an outsider within my own family, so I was able to quickly adapt. When I was seventeen, I went to the Club Manhattan, a bustling, smoke-filled music venue, where I met two men who would play important roles in my life.

The first was Raymond Hill, a talented sax player with whom I had a brief romance that produced my beloved son Craig. The second was Ike Turner, a musician and bandleader who was famous for his groundbreaking song, "Rocket 88."

Ike spotted me at the Club Manhattan and invited me to sing with his band. He became a mentor to me and launched my musical career. I was thrilled. There I was, a teenager, standing onstage, dressed in fine clothes, singing my heart out. I never imagined that kind of career was possible for me. It seemed like a dream come true, until it wasn't.

Against my better judgment, Ike became my first husband. The best thing our relationship produced was my second beloved son, Ronnie. Ike and I also raised his two sons from his first marriage, Ike Jr. and Michael, so I was a mother of four when I was still figuring out how to be an adult.

Living with Ike was a challenging series of ordeals. He changed my name from Anna Mae Bullock to Tina Turner in the early days of our relationship, despite my protests. After that, during our difficult ascent to fame in the 1960s as the Ike & Tina Turner Revue, I suffered years of domestic violence, both emotional and physical. Busted lips, black eyes, dislocated joints, broken bones, and psychological torture became a part of everyday life. I got used to suffering and tried to keep myself sane while somehow managing his insanity. I felt there was no way out.

By the mid-1960s, we had achieved success with some of our songs, and my 1966 solo "River Deep–Mountain High," produced by Phil Spector, was a smash in the United Kingdom and Europe. Thanks to that hit, the Rolling Stones invited us to tour overseas with them in the fall of 1966, which was another dream come true.

However, after we returned to the States, life with Ike got worse. The pressure to turn out hits intensified Ike's insecurities and fueled his drug dependency, making his bouts of violence more frequent.

I began to lose hope.

Finally, in 1968, I was so depressed and despondent that I couldn't think straight. Ike's abuse and infidelities left me numb, unable to feel for myself or my family, unable to feel alive. The only thing I could feel was that I had reached the end. One night before I was set to go onstage, I attempted suicide by taking fifty sleeping pills. People backstage noticed something was very wrong with me and rushed me to the hospital, which saved my life.

At first, I was disappointed when I woke up and realized I was still alive. I thought death was my only chance at escape. But it was not in my nature to stay down for long. For nearly twenty-nine years, I'd always found a way to get up and go on, despite all the trials in my life. In fact, that was my mantra before I even knew what a mantra was. "I'll go on."

This time, too, I tried to pull myself out of despair as best I could. If this was my lot in life, I thought, I would somehow make the most of it. Then, it occurred to me that maybe I had survived for a reason, for some greater purpose. From that point on, no matter how tough life was, my instinct, my heart, told me to just keep going.

Where was I headed? That was still unclear.

Never underestimate the power of dreams,
and the influence of the human spirit...
The potential for greatness lives within each of us.
—WILMA RUDOLPH

•

When you can't find your direction,
and your heart won't guide you home,
let go, and let God...
Nam-myoho-renge-kyo,
Nam-myoho-renge-kyo,
Nam-myoho-renge-kyo.

—OLIVIA NEWTON-JOHN, "LET GO LET GOD"

The early 1970s were a difficult time, both personally and professionally. We hadn't had any significant success with our music in recent years, so I took it upon myself to do something about it. I wanted to write a song. I had been helping a songwriter who worked with us, cleaning up his writing, and I thought, if he could write songs, so could I.

Over the years, I'd heard songwriters say, "Write what you know." Following that advice, my first try was a song I penned in 1973, called "Nutbush City Limits," about the place where I was born. It was a hit, especially in Europe. That relieved some of our financial worries, and it made me so happy to think I could do something creative. But the kids and I were still suffering at home, where we were always at the mercy of Ike's mood and temper.

I was often distraught and exhausted from the abuse, and it was getting harder to hide it from the people around me, who weren't blind to my problems. When I was alone with them, they'd sometimes try to speak with me about it, saying things like "I hope you're taking care of yourself." I knew it was their way of saying, "Why don't you get the heck out of that mess?"

One day, our sound engineer said something different to me. "Tina, you should try chanting. It will help you change your life."

I didn't know exactly what chanting was, and I didn't ask for an explanation. Wasn't chanting something hippies did? I soon forgot about it.

A couple of months later, my youngest son, Ronnie, came home carrying what looked like a lacquered brown wooden rosary. He said excitedly, "Mother, these are Buddhist chanting beads. If you chant Nam-myoho-renge-kyo, you can have anything you want."

What? How could I ever have anything I want? I didn't even know how to process that statement.

"It's mystical, but it all makes sense," he assured me. "I just can't explain it. Let's go up the street to a chanting meeting and learn more."

Under normal circumstances I might have gone. But by that time, I was basically a prisoner in my own home; I couldn't go anywhere without Ike's permission. He rarely allowed me to go on my own to places other than the grocery store or the recording studio. So, I told Ronnie he could invite the Buddhist people to visit us, but I couldn't go to them. That was my second brush with chanting, but nothing came of it.

A few weeks later, Ike brought home a cheerful-looking woman to meet me. He was always parading people through our house to "see Tina." Out of nowhere, she started talking about chanting. She was a Buddhist.

Apparently, the universe was trying very hard to send me an important message. This time, I was ready to listen.

Chapter Two

THE WORLDS WITHIN US

It was another typically beautiful day in Southern California—the kind you see on postcards, with blue skies and plenty of sunshine. But it wasn't a typical day for me because I had heard about chanting for the third time in as many months and I couldn't stop thinking about it.

It was 1973, and I was approaching my thirty-fourth birthday, doing my best to raise four strong-willed teenage boys while dealing with a litany of relationship and professional problems. No matter how intense the stress became, I kept all the pressure inside. This was a bad time; yet somehow, I felt a spark of hope.

I had seen enough of life to believe there's no such thing as a coincidence. I believe that our situations, good or bad, always happen for a reason, even when the reasons elude us. Still, I wondered why I had to suffer abuse and negativity when I had done nothing to deserve it. Not in this lifetime, anyway.

But no matter what happened, I tried to be a good person. If there was any justice in the universe, I hoped some long-overdue positivity would come my way. Maybe this was my moment. Three people who didn't know one another, and were of different ages, genders, and ethnicities, had each offered the same advice about changing my life for the better. They told me: "Learn about Buddhist wisdom and start to chant."

I felt this message had come to me for a reason.

All I wanted was a way to change my life. Even the slightest improvement would be a relief.

I should try chanting and test it out, I told myself.

I began by reading books on the subject by Daisaku Ikeda, a true thought leader in Buddhist practice. Although I hadn't been a great student in my younger years, I was a curious person who always enjoyed learning. As I grew older, books became good friends to me, transporting me to other places and introducing me to new ideas. Whether I was reading about fashion, the history of ancient Egypt, science, or politics, I welcomed the opportunity to improve myself.

Ikeda's writings whisked me away to a mystical era in ancient India, where I learned about a concept called the Ten Worlds.

A colorful, practical principle of Buddhist wisdom, with

origins dating back nearly three thousand years, the Ten Worlds describes ten categories of our "life condition"—our ever-changing moods, thoughts, and general states of being—that powerfully influence our emotions, our actions, and our view of ourselves and others.

These ten "worlds" are actually life states that we all experience internally, and they range from the very worst to the very best of human behavior. The lesser of these inner conditions—when left unexamined, or unchecked—can lead to habits that trap us in unhealthy patterns. That's certainly what happened to me.

By becoming conscious of these conditions, I was able to see the tendencies that were holding me back and bringing me down, including low self-esteem, codependence, denying my worth, and deferring decisions about my life to others. If I could see these aspects of myself more clearly, I could begin to change them, opening the way for me to build lasting success and happiness.

To help illustrate the Ten Worlds, I invite you to come with me on a quick journey. Fast-forward from 1973, when I was first learning about Buddhism, to a lazy Sunday morning in 1977. It was a few years after I started chanting, and the first full year of my life as a single, independent woman.

As anyone who knows me well can tell you, I love to sleep. After all those years of performing, I'm a night owl, and sometimes I like to sleep quite late in the mornings.

That Sunday morning in 1977 was no different.

No one can figure out
your worth
but you.
—PEARL BAILEY

•

The challenge is not to be perfect.
It's to be whole.
—JANE FONDA

•

We don't see things as they are;
we see them as we are.
—ANAÏS NIN

Happily asleep in my bed, I'm awakened by the annoying sound of my alarm clock. I wonder: *Why did I set that today? Nothing's going on. It's Sunday.*

With one eye half open, I push the off button and drift back to dreamland.

Then, a distant thought bubbles up from the recesses of my mind, jolting me awake with this sobering fact: Today is actually Monday, and now I'm late for a rehearsal with Cher for her television show.

I splash water on my face, spray myself with perfume, and throw on the clothes I wore last night, which are conveniently draped on a chair right where I left them. My stomach is growling, so I grab an apple and run out the door.

Traffic is jammed, making me even later, and my temper is starting to flare. I turn on the radio, hoping for some musical relief, as Barbra Streisand's gorgeous ballad "Evergreen" comes on, calming my nerves.

Arriving late to CBS Television City, which is unlike me, I'm thankful that no one mentions my tardiness. Everyone seems happy to see me.

My embarrassment at being late quickly gives way to delight when our brilliant costume designer, Bob Mackie, shows me a sparkly creation he's made for me to wear on the show. I've been wanting exactly this kind of costume for years, and now I'm thrilled that my desire's been fulfilled.

The rehearsal is fun and easy. Cher and I always have a

good time together. After a quick bite at the nearby Farmers Market, I head out to meet some friends who've invited me to chant with them.

Feeling much happier than I did this morning, I'm more like my usual self as I steer my Jaguar XKE Roadster, which I cherish and *love* driving.

To my surprise, I'm suddenly pulled over by a police officer. I'm not aware that I've done anything wrong, so I'm feeling nervous. I try to suppress feelings of angst and indignation, remembering what I know about injustices at the hands of policemen.

These thoughts evaporate when the officer politely asks, "How are you doing today, ma'am?" I tell him I'm fine, and on my way to a Buddhist chanting meeting. The expression on his face indicates he was not expecting to hear that. "Is there some urgent rush to get there?" he asks. "Because you rolled right through that last stop sign just now."

Turns out the reason I'm being stopped is because of the hard-to-break habit of "California stops." If you've never heard of a California stop, it's when the wheels of your car don't actually come to a complete halt at a stop sign.

I apologize and explain that I'm not the best driver in the world, and my thoughts have been distracted by some family drama lately. The officer reminds me to always halt fully at stop signs and red lights and lets me off with a warning. Then, I'm back on the road.

While driving (a lot more carefully than I did before being stopped), I listen to a fascinating interview on public radio with scientist Carl Sagan. His comments reveal things I never knew about the universe, leading me to think about my place in the world.

As I wait to turn a corner near a retirement home, I see an older woman whose smile reminds me of my dear grandmother Mama Georgie. Something about this moment makes me resolve that I'll spend more time doing good things for others, the way she taught me to do.

Thank you, Mama Georgie, I think to myself as I send her a loving prayer of appreciation.

Why am I telling you all the details of a seemingly unremarkable day in Los Angeles? Because, during this time, you traveled with me through eight of the Ten Worlds, and we went all the way from "Hunger" to "Bodhisattva."

Since ancient times, the Ten Worlds have been described (from lowest to highest) as Hell, Hunger, Animality, Anger, Tranquility, Heaven, Learning, Realization, Bodhisattva, and Buddhahood.

The first four of these worlds can be summed up like this: the state of suffering or destructive despair (Hell), the state of being controlled by insatiable desires (Hunger), the state of being swayed by instinctive behaviors (Animality), and the state of ego attachments, dominated by conflict and arrogance (Anger).

The fifth and sixth worlds are the state of relative calm

(Tranquility) and the state of temporary elation at the gratification of a desire (Heaven).

Together, these six states of being, from Hell to Heaven, are considered the lower paths, since their emergence, or disappearance, is determined mostly by the way we react to external circumstances. Any satisfaction we may gain while experiencing these life conditions depends on temporary, external situations, so it doesn't last long.

In contrast, the remaining four worlds are the higher paths, which require our conscious, inner effort to manifest them. The gains we make while experiencing these higher conditions are long-lasting.

In Buddhist texts, these four higher paths are often called the four noble paths.

The first two of these four higher paths are the state of seeking truth from the teachings or experiences of others (Learning) and the state of understanding truth through our own efforts and observations (Realization). Achieving these life conditions gives us some independence from the ups and downs of the lower paths.

Then we come to the highest two paths.

The first of these two is the state of compassion, altruism, and aspiring to enlightenment while finding joy in helping others do the same (Bodhisattva).

Finally, we have the highest condition in life. This is the state of total freedom, wholeness, and absolute happiness, in which we can enjoy a limitless sense of unity with the life force of the universe itself (Buddhahood). I like to think of this as an indestructible, diamond-like condition—a treasure we have deep within our hearts.

We reveal this greatest of life conditions through our concerted positive actions, particularly those actions we take while we're in the state of Bodhisattva. The state of Buddhahood overflows with boundless compassion, infinite wisdom, and steadfast courage.

We all have the potential to manifest any of these ten conditions at any moment, and as we are experiencing one of them, the other nine conditions remain dormant.

As the example of my memorable day in 1977 shows, we all experience swings from one life condition, or world, to another, and we may go through many different conditions in a single day. At any given moment, we are always experiencing one of these conditions, and the qualities of that condition inside ourselves reflect outward into every area of our lives.

When I was growing up, I wasn't aware that the qualities of Buddhahood existed. During my childhood, my home environment revolved mostly around the lower four or five worlds. Occasionally, there were times when I briefly experienced Heaven, such as when I went to the movies or visited with my beloved Mama Georgie. Later, in school, I experienced the states of Learning and Realization, expanding my horizons with new subjects and class activities, but those states were irregular and brief.

The externals are simply so many props;
everything we need is within us.
—ETTY HILLESUM

•

Knowing yourself is
the beginning of all wisdom.
—ARISTOTLE

•

The mind is its own place, and in itself
can make a Heaven of Hell, a Hell of Heaven.
—JOHN MILTON

As a teenager, I took a job working for the Hendersons, a kind young white family, who opened my eyes to what it was like to be a part of a happy home. For the first time, I saw what a higher life condition could be. I felt their compassion and desire to help me in the way they taught me social manners and told me about the world outside of Tennessee. Thanks to the Hendersons, I observed the condition of Bodhisattva, and I aspired to have the sort of positivity I saw in their lives.

Though I was becoming aware that higher life states were possible, I didn't know how to achieve them. I hadn't yet found a way to transform my state of life.

But I carried these memories with me as a guiding light.

Later, I worked as a nurse's assistant at a hospital. Let me tell you, if there's one building on Earth where all of the Ten Worlds are manifesting at the same time, it's a hospital. There are people experiencing genuine emergencies, as well as nervous hypochondriacs, people waiting to donate blood, people doing important research to cure disease, babies crying their first cries, loved ones saying their final goodbyes, and everything in between. That was a mind-opening experience, too.

Now that we're familiar with the range of life conditions, let's revisit our journey through that day of mine in 1977, only this time through the lens of the Ten Worlds.

Sleeping snugly in my bed, I am in a state of Tranquility.

As the alarm sounds, instinctive reflexes, and perhaps momentary fear, trigger Animality. The notion that I'm safe to go back to sleep for as long as I want is Heaven, which is soon shattered when I remember it's Monday. Disbelief turns to Anger, as I berate myself for oversleeping.

Now, you might interpret my feeling hungry on the way out the door as the state of Hunger, but it's more accurately Animality, since it's instinctive, in contrast to the actual state of Hunger, which is about our desires or greed (not literally wanting something to eat).

The traffic jams bring out Anger again, but soothing music helps me settle back to Tranquility.

The realization of something I've been wanting for so long (Hunger), a gorgeous Bob Mackie costume, brings out Heaven, although this is a temporary high.

Back in my car, I return to Tranquility until a police officer stops me, which briefly brings out Anger. Fortunately, he lets me go with only a warning, and Tranquility returns.

Listening to Carl Sagan's insights on public radio gives rise to Learning and Realization. To cap off the day, remembering my grandmother and her lessons about helping others immediately brings out the state of Bodhisattva.

Now that I'm ending my day in a higher life condition, the things that seemed bad earlier in the day don't seem so bad anymore. But those external circumstances haven't changed—it's my life condition that changed. My life condition colors my view of the whole day, past and present.

In other words, our life condition can brighten, or darken, our feelings about the same circumstances.

If you cannot find peace within yourself,
you will never find it anywhere else.
—MARVIN GAYE

•

I believe in the soul . . . I believe it is prompt
accountability for one's choices, a willing acceptance
of responsibility for one's thoughts, behavior,
and actions that makes it powerful.
—ALICE WALKER

•

The ultimate mystery is one's own self.
—SAMMY DAVIS JR.

Although the details may be different, I'm sure you've experienced similar situations, and you know that feeling of being on a roller-coaster ride through many different life conditions in a single day.

The more I've learned about modern psychology, the more I see its similarities to ancient Buddhist wisdom. I even found that Abraham Maslow's well-known theory of self-actualization and the hierarchy of needs have been likened to the Ten Worlds. The first time I saw Maslow's hierarchy of needs drawn as levels in a pyramid, I was struck by its resemblance to Buddhist levels of life conditions.

Maslow's theory says that people naturally seek to satisfy their basic needs in the following order, from lower to higher:

First there is the physical level of our basic survival needs (food, water, and shelter); then comes the level of safety (security, health, and finances); and the level of psychological needs of belonging (love, friendship, and family). These first three levels in Maslow's pyramid correspond to the six lower life conditions of the Ten Worlds.

For example, if we are struggling to meet our basic physical and safety needs, we're likely to experience the conditions of Hell, Hunger, Anger, and Animality. And when our psychological needs are met, we achieve Tranquility and Heaven.

In Maslow's pyramid, the next level is esteem (accomplishment, freedom, and self-confidence), which corresponds to Learning and Realization; and finally, there is the level of self-actualization (fulfillment of potential, discovery of purpose, and clarity of perception), which shares elements of the life conditions of Bodhisattva and Buddhahood.

When we seek to self-actualize—when we aspire to manifest the states of Bodhisattva and Buddhahood—we are changed for the better. I spoke about this often while touring Japan in the late 1980s, explaining that, thanks to my Buddhist practice, I felt like a different person had emerged from within me, my true self, with a strong sense of purpose and self-awareness.

Despite the similarities between the Ten Worlds and Maslow's hierarchy, there is a key difference. Unlike the stages that one must satisfy in order to move on to the next level on Maslow's pyramid, the optimistic message of Buddhism is that each of the Ten Worlds contains the potential of all the other life conditions within itself. In other words, we can move directly from one condition to any other, without having to experience an intermediate condition.

This concept is liberating because it tells us that even if we are experiencing the condition of Hell, we have the potential to instantly manifest any of the higher states, even Buddhahood.

For example, people who have survived a natural disaster report experiencing profound insights about the interrelatedness of all living things. They often feel more compassionate, and at one with the universe.

This awareness of our potential to elevate ourselves out of the lowest depths of suffering to the highest state of human existence is life changing. Armed with this knowledge, we see that there is a positive quality in every condition, so we don't need to fear any state of life. When we wake up to this reality, that any condition we may be experiencing possesses the potential for all other states of being, we can find the light of hope no matter what our circumstances are.

This understanding is crucial, because without hope, anything can become a source of despair. With hope, anything can become a source of joy.

We can also be confident that we can use any of the lower conditions of life as fuel to achieve the higher ones. This is our human superpower, the ability to "change poison into medicine."

Thanks to my Buddhist practice, the empowering process of changing poison into medicine—transforming destructive negativity into creative positivity—has become the hope-filled theme of my life, which we'll explore more in chapter five.

In the meantime, know that whenever you feel your life condition diving down into the lower worlds, you can lift yourself up. Sometimes you can do it through relatively simple efforts. Focusing your mind, doing yoga, running, swimming, working out, practicing breathing exercises, taking a walk, "shaking it off," or, as many of us learned in kindergarten, stopping for a time-out or nap can sometimes work wonders. If these methods aren't effective at raising your state of mind, you can explore other ways, such as prayer, chanting, meditation, or study. Choose whatever path works best for you.

In my case, until I was thirty-four, nothing I tried seemed to make a lasting improvement in my life condition. Nothing helped me to lift myself out of the lower worlds. I was stuck in negative cycles, silently suffering, unsure how I could ever make my dreams come true.

Then, I began to chant. Buddhism taught me how to access a direct path upward in my life condition, a spiritual express lane, so to speak, by chanting Nam-myoho-renge-kyo.

I think most people who know something about me have probably heard that I study and practice Buddhism and that I chant Nam-myoho-renge-kyo. I'll bet fewer people know how chanting actually works.

Now that we've explored the Ten Worlds together, we'll look at what the words—or sounds—*Nam-myoho-renge-kyo* mean, both literally and to me personally. I'd like to share with you some of the wondrous ways in which chanting has helped me to become happy and strong, how it lifted my life condition—and how it can do the same for you.

HIGHLIGHTS OF POSITIVE AND NEGATIVE ASPECTS IN EACH OF THE TEN WORLDS

1. HELL

Positive: Personal experiences of deep suffering can lead us to the desire to help others find their way out of their own suffering.

Negative: Hopeless despair; the inability to see oneself and others clearly; self-destructive tendencies.

•

2. HUNGER

Positive: Aiming to achieve goals; yearning to have more.

Negative: Greed; hedonism; insatiable desires.

•

3. ANIMALITY

Positive: Healthy instincts to survive and to protect and nurture life.

Negative: Acting only from instinct; threatening the weak and fearing the strong.

•

4. ANGER

Positive: Righteous passion to fight injustice; creative force for change.

Negative: Egotistic self-righteousness; destructive competitiveness; conflict.

5. TRANQUILITY

Positive: Neutral state of peacefulness;
ability to act with humane reason.

Negative: State of passive inactivity;
unwillingness to tackle problems; laziness.

•

6. HEAVEN

Positive: Sense of pleasure and happiness; heightened
awareness; feelings of appreciation for being alive.

Negative: Short-lived elation that is typically self-oriented;
wish for fleeting gratification to repeat can lead to excess.

•

7. LEARNING

Positive: Striving for self-improvement by studying
new concepts through others' teachings.

Negative: Tendency to become self-centered; dismissive
attitude toward others with less experience or knowledge.

•

8. REALIZATION

Positive: Gaining wisdom and insight through one's
own learning and personal observation of the world.

Negative: Lacking a broad view of life due to self-
absorption; feelings of superiority over others.

9. BODHISATTVA

This word contains *bodhi,* or "enlightenment," and *sattva,* or "living beings"—meaning one who seeks enlightenment for oneself and others.

Positive: Compassion; acting selflessly for others without expectation of reward.

Negative: Neglecting one's own life; feeling contempt for those one tries to help.

•

10. BUDDHAHOOD

This word indicates the state of enlightenment to the ultimate reality of the universe and all workings of life.

Positive: Boundless wisdom, courage, and compassion; a grand life force that illuminates the positive aspects of each of the other nine worlds. Buddhahood is the only life condition that has no negative aspects.

Chapter Three

ANTHEM OF ANGELS

The fragrance of flowers perfumed my spring garden today as I looked across the shimmering waters of Lake Zürich. I smiled as I began my morning prayers, realizing it's been nearly half a century since I first chanted Nam-myoho-renge-kyo.

The transformation in my life from where I was upon first hearing these words to where I am today, as I write this, is extraordinary. If I hadn't made the journey myself, it might seem like a fairy tale. Yet that's exactly what I did—I made my dreams, my own vision of a fairy tale, come true.

Whatever your dreams may be, I know you can make them come true, too.

My wish for you is to succeed and achieve your own definition of happiness, however you paint that picture. If you take away anything from these pages, I hope that my story of self-actualization will inform and inspire your dreams, now and in the future.

When I speak of dreams coming true, I'm not referring to the external desires in our lives. Material rewards are lovely, and I'm deeply grateful for all the wonderful things in my life now. I worked hard to get to where I am today. But that isn't the transformation I'm talking about. What shifted for me, what enabled me to attain all the conspicuous benefits I enjoy, was infinitely more important—the deep, inner changes that resulted from my spiritual practice of chanting, studying, and helping others.

When I first received the gift of Nam-myoho-renge-kyo, it marked the beginning of a new life for me in more ways than I could have imagined. Thanks to the spiritual awakenings I experienced by chanting, I gained the clarity and strength to make countless important changes in my life.

It all started when I had that series of encounters with people who urged me to chant. Fortunately, I listened to the message that was trying so hard to reach me. I began by chanting a little each day, sometimes just saying Nam-myoho-renge-kyo a few times in a row. Then I started chanting five minutes a day, then fifteen, and noticed small, yet definite, improvements and shifts in my life condition.

For example, I found a rare cache of my favorite makeup that had been discontinued, and I often felt like I hit long stretches of green lights when I drove. Bit by bit, my Buddhist practice was helping me to rearrange my place in the universe.

Soon, I increased my chanting to a half hour, sometimes an hour.

Although I wanted to chant with my sangha, the local community of practitioners, I was still married to Ike, and he was afraid of my chanting because he thought I might be able to put a curse on him or something. I realize now that he mostly feared the person I could become through my spiritual practice. His hold on me was threatened because chanting strengthened me.

He almost never let me go out to meet people without him, so I found time whenever I could to chant secretly, stealing precious moments to do my prayers morning and night. Sometimes, a few of my brave chanting friends, Susie Sempers, Valerie Bishop, and Maria Lucien, would sneak into the house to practice with me when my husband wasn't around.

Gradually, I felt I was getting in sync, in rhythm with life on the deepest level. The more I chanted, the more I felt my true self, my inherent Buddha nature, awakening. My life condition kept rising, and I developed a newfound feeling of detachment around my husband. I became so strong inside that eventually our conflicts began to feel like a game, like some sort of karmic test.

In the midst of chaos, I felt as if I had been reborn.

The brighter my inner light shined, the more my environment improved, and dreams I hadn't even expressed outside of my chanting began to come true. Internal gains were followed by other benefits, starting a positive cycle that grew over time. The first big example of this was powerful. I had always wanted to act in film, and out of the blue, I was asked to star in the rock opera film *Tommy,* together with Elton John, Ann-Margret, Roger Daltrey, Eric Clapton, and Jack Nicholson. Remember my love of movies when I was a child? This was a real dream come true.

Slowly but surely, I increased my Buddhist practice over the next couple of years. I became stronger—so strong that in the summer of 1976, I finally found the courage to run away from Ike, to escape from the unhealthy domestic situation I had been trapped in for so long, and I filed for divorce.

Once I gained my independence, I also gained the freedom to go to chanting meetings whenever I pleased. All around the world there are neighborhood chanting meetings organized by the Soka Gakkai International (SGI) Buddhist network; warm and friendly gatherings of people who chant Nam-myoho-renge-kyo. I joined the meetings nearest me, in the Brentwood area of West Los Angeles.

Oh, how I enjoyed studying and practicing Buddhism with other openminded people. What a relief and delight that was! After years of oppression at home, having the freedom to express my thoughts and beliefs was sheer joy. Looking back on it now, it seems like such a simple thing. But those of us who have survived abusive and codependent relationships know the value of basic pleasures and rights that others may take for granted.

In West LA, I also discovered that a number of musicians, including my friends Ana Maria and Wayne Shorter (the jazz genius), hosted chanting meetings. Ana and I had first met one night in a New York City nightclub long before I'd heard about Buddhism. Wayne was performing at the same place where I was doing a gig, and Ana and I befriended each other backstage.

Even though we'd been friends for a while, I didn't know that Ana and Wayne practiced Buddhism until I started practicing myself. When I went to tell Ana how much I loved chanting, thinking I was sharing with her something she'd find new and interesting, she replied with a smile and a big hug, saying: "Darling, we've been chanting for years!"

Ana later told me: "When we became friends in New York, I sensed a deep sadness in you and felt you were hiding something about your situation." Even without her knowing my problems, she said, "Since we first met, I've had your name in my prayer book and have been chanting for your true happiness."

Hearing her heartfelt words gave me chills and brought tears to my eyes. It was another sign that I was exactly where I was meant to be—I had found my sacred space, my beloved community of spirit.

As I was beginning my daily chanting practice, I was amazed to discover that someone I'd always admired, Mahatma Gandhi, opened the daily prayer meetings at his ashram by chanting Nam-myoho-renge-kyo with his disciples.

There is an indefinable mysterious power
that pervades everything...
an orderliness in the universe...
an unalterable law governing everything and
every being that exists or lives. It is no blind law,
for no blind law can govern the conduct of living beings.
—MAHATMA GANDHI

·

What unites us is far greater than what divides us
as families and friends...
and spiritual sojourners on this Earth.
—MARIAN WRIGHT EDELMAN

But the story of Nam-myoho-renge-kyo began long before me, or Gandhi. It started more than 2,500 years ago with a wise man named Shakyamuni. In the West, Shakyamuni is more commonly known as Siddhartha Gautama, the historical Buddha. I love reading stories that teach the history of Buddhism. My prayer room is filled with books that shed light on the subject, and I want to share with you some of what I've learned.

Shakyamuni was born a prince in northern India (what is now Nepal), and his name means "sage of the Shakya clan" in Sanskrit, which was the ancient language of his land. Although he grew up in luxury, at the age of nineteen he discovered that the people outside his palace walls were suffering. He then renounced his pampered royal status and set out on his own to experience the harsh realities of everyday life among the people.

Shakyamuni dedicated himself to a spiritual quest, seeking to understand the mysteries of what he perceived as humanity's four inescapable sufferings: birth, sickness, aging, and death. After surviving many ordeals, practicing austerities, and meditating for nearly ten years, he found enlightenment while seated beneath a magnificent bodhi tree. Thus, at age thirty, he became known as a Buddha.

The term *Buddha* means "enlightened one." When a person is unclear about the workings of the universe, they are a deluded, ordinary person; but when they achieve clarity into the nature of all life, then they are a Buddha.

Having achieved enlightenment, Shakyamuni dedicated the next forty years of his life to sharing his revelations, traveling great distances to help relieve the suffering he saw everywhere. To spread his message, he prepared his disciples by teaching them more simplistic concepts and gradually built up to his ultimate revelations, just like we must learn basic arithmetic before moving on to geometry and more complicated forms of mathematics.

The wisdom Shakyamuni shared was compiled into "sutras," which are collections of teachings and lectures. The Sanskrit word *sutra* means "thread," indicating a weaving together of wisdom to create literary tapestries of enlightenment.

During the final eight years of Shakyamuni's life, he taught his ultimate revelations, encompassed in the Lotus Sutra.

Although the wisdom of the Lotus Sutra may be new to many in the West, a couple of American writers—Henry David Thoreau and Ralph Waldo Emerson—were actually responsible for first introducing the Lotus Sutra to much of the Western world in the nineteenth century.

"The Preaching of Buddha" was the name they gave to excerpts from the Lotus Sutra that they published in the January 1844 edition of *The Dial,* a quarterly journal based in Boston.

Thoreau helped translate the text into English from an earlier French translation, and Emerson served as editor. It's well known that Emerson was a student of Eastern wisdom, and his publication of excerpts from the Lotus Sutra was another sign of his eagerness to share with Western society what he had learned.

Today, the Lotus Sutra is the most recognized sutra in the world. It is the basis of many Buddhist schools of thought that spread throughout Asia over the 2,500 years since Shakyamuni.

Like Christianity and other major world religions, Buddhism can be seen as an ancient tree with many denominational branches. Among them is the Soka Gakkai tradition of Buddhism that I practice. This tradition originated with the teachings of a religious reformer and philosopher named Nichiren in thirteenth-century Japan.

Nichiren lived during a time of terrible social unrest and natural catastrophes. Born into a family of fishermen, he was interested in philosophy from childhood.

At the age of twelve, he devoted his life to study and began researching the vast wealth of Buddhist scriptures. For two decades, Nichiren sought to clarify the essence of Buddhism and to simplify its practice, leading the way to Buddhahood for anyone, regardless of life condition or circumstances.

Nichiren taught that chanting Nam-myoho-renge-kyo is the essence of the Lotus Sutra. He dedicated his life to teaching people that this simple practice of chanting Nam-myoho-renge-kyo contains the entirety of Buddhist teachings and can open the door to enlightenment for all.

Today, chanting Nam-myoho-renge-kyo is one of the best-known and most widely embraced Buddhist practices around the globe. At any given moment, day or night, various people all around the world are chanting, including me.

Some people say Nam-myoho-renge-kyo is like a song. In the Soka Gakkai tradition, we are taught how to sing it. When I first attended an SGI chanting meeting and heard a group of people chanting together in rhythmic unity, the energy was so beautiful and strong that I felt goodness all around me and a sense of joyous eternity.

I was profoundly moved and I thought to myself, *Nam-myoho-renge-kyo is the anthem of angels.*

So, why do I and millions of others chant?

The simplest answer is this: to become the embodiment of happiness.

In every corner of every country I've visited in my travels, there is one thing I know that all people have in common: the desire for lasting happiness.

Everyone wants to be happy. The search for happiness is a core instinct that transcends creed and culture. Everything people say or do is ultimately rooted in the belief, albeit often subconscious, that their actions will lead to happiness.

The trick is how to make happiness last. Happiness is a feeling. And, like all feelings, it can disappear as quickly as it appears.

True and lasting happiness is elusive. I know all about that.

We are stardust
We are golden
And we've got to get ourselves
Back to the garden
—JONI MITCHELL, "WOODSTOCK"

•

What you do makes a difference,
and you have to decide what kind of difference
you want to make.
—JANE GOODALL

•

Spread love everywhere you go.
Let no one ever come to you
without leaving happier.
—MOTHER TERESA

Despite working my way from hardscrabble beginnings to international recognition, I had moments, even in the best of times, when I felt as if something was missing. My karma, my karmic limitations, were invisible chains pulling me backward. I'm sure you've heard the word *karma* before, but what is karma exactly?

Karma is a Sanskrit word that means "action." Think of karma as the sum of all your actions—thoughts, words, and deeds—from the eternal past to the present moment and on into the future, as you continue to create new actions. Karma is a balance sheet, so to speak, of your negative and positive acts throughout time, without any beginning or end.

Our karma determines our dominant life condition. Karma is why we sometimes find ourselves stuck, seemingly unable to break through challenges, or why we face repeated patterns of things we don't want, or why we seem to be unable to rise up from lower to higher life conditions. These limitations all result from our own actions, our karma.

One way to think of karmic limitations, which are typically invisible to the eye, is to compare karma to gravity. The pull of gravity, like the pull of karma, is invisible yet constantly influences everything we do.

And yet, science has found ways to escape from the gravitational pull of Earth. I like astrophysicist Neil deGrasse Tyson's simple explanations of this. He said that to escape gravity, we must move at a speed greater than its force can resist. This speed is known as cosmic "escape velocity." Every object in the universe has one. On Earth, that velocity is about seven miles per second.

This means that in order to break out of gravity's pull, you must leave the Earth's surface with a force so great it can propel you at least seven miles per second.

I think of karma in a similar way.

To free yourself from the invisible ties of karma, to achieve "karmic escape velocity," you must increase the power of your life force until it becomes greater than the force of karmic pull.

Now, some karma is light, like gravity on the moon. (Lunar escape velocity is only one-sixth that of Earth.)

Other karma is heavy and can feel inescapable, which is exactly how my circumstances felt for so long. Heavy karma can feel like the pull of a massive black hole that yanks everything into its destructive abyss.

To escape the pull of a black hole in space, you would need to travel faster than the speed of light. Yet, as Albert Einstein taught us, nothing in space can move faster than light, and thus you'd be helplessly stuck.

In the case of a karmic black hole, however, your life force can definitely achieve a velocity greater than the speed of light—let's call it the velocity of enlightenment.

By increasing your spiritual velocity of enlightenment, you can break free from the gravitational pull of any karmic limitation.

My life is proof of this.

Stretch your mind and fly.
—WHITNEY M. YOUNG JR.

•

The most beautiful thing we can
experience is the mysterious.
—ALBERT EINSTEIN

•

O friend, understand:
the body
is like the ocean,
rich with hidden treasures.
Open your innermost chamber and light its lamp.
—MIRABAI

Sometimes, breaking free from the pull of negative karma doesn't require an outward change, but rather an inner one—a change of heart, a shift in perception. For as we know from the Ten Worlds, the quality of our life condition—whether high or low—can cause us to make the best of the worst, or the worst of the best.

That's where the power of chanting Nam-myoho-renge-kyo comes in.

The concise meaning of Nam-myoho-renge-kyo is: "Devotion to the Mystic Law of the Lotus Sutra."

A more intricate meaning of this phrase is revealed by looking at each of its elements:

Nam
Pronounced with a soft *a* like the *a* in *father*

Myo
Sounds like adding an *m* to the first half of *yo-yo*

Ho
Pronounced the same as the garden tool *hoe*

Ren
Sounds like the bird *wren*

Ge
Like the word *get* without the *t*

Kyo
Like adding a *k* to the first half of *yo-yo*

Nam means "devoting oneself."

Myoho means "Mystic Law," with *myo* indicating life's mystic essence, and *ho* representing its manifestations. *Myoho* expresses the fundamental life force of the universe.

Next, *renge* means "lotus flower," expressing cause and effect, since lotus plants bring forth their blossoms and seed-pods simultaneously.

Renge also indicates the Lotus Sutra.

Finally, *kyo* has multiple layers of significance, including the teachings of Buddha and sound vibration.

Nam-myoho-renge-kyo can be more colorfully interpreted as: "I devote myself to the universal Mystic Law of cause and effect through the sound vibration of Buddha wisdom."

Think of the act of chanting Nam-myoho-renge-kyo as a kind of spiritual workout. You've probably noticed that some people only need to work out a little to stay in good physical shape, while others need to exercise a lot to stay fit. I believe it's the same for spiritual fitness.

Depending on our unique circumstances, predominant life condition, and karmic patterns, the effort we must exert to stay in a spiritually strong place differs. It also differs depending on our goals, and on the kinds of changes we're looking to make.

While I was facing the hardest challenges of my life, I was also dreaming the biggest dreams I ever imagined, and I was chanting several hours a day to achieve them. When I mention how much I chanted during those toughest days, people gasp and say they couldn't possibly find the will or the time to do anything for several hours a day. That's understandable and absolutely fine.

Maybe fifteen or thirty minutes would be the ideal amount of daily chanting for you. Chanting to your heart's content is what's most important, and any amount of chanting is beneficial. It's all up to you.

For me, chanting several hours a day during those difficult years was invigorating. I could feel the positive differences that chanting made in my life, which motivated me to chant even more. It just seemed like common sense to me. How could I not want to do more of something that improved my life so dramatically?

I compare it to the preparation required to win an athletic contest. In my heart, I had decided to go for the gold in a spiritual Olympics, but my starting place wouldn't have qualified for a junior varsity team. I had to work harder to compensate for my handicaps.

If you imagine the discipline required to get from where I was to where I wanted to go, then it's easy to understand why my practice was so extensive in those days. Over the years, as my life condition rose and my circumstances improved, my practice shifted to more moderate levels.

Whether I chant for minutes or hours, I have always loved my daily routine of chanting. This is how I saved myself. This is how I made my wildest dreams come true.

Whatever methods you use to improve your life, the

most important thing to remember is that these efforts will strengthen you and give you the power to break free from your karmic limitations, elevate yourself to the higher worlds, and build the life you want.

When we dream, and especially when we dream big, there is always a gap between the reality of what we have and our goals. The key is finding a way to successfully bridge that distance.

My spiritual practice is what bridged the gap for me. Hard work, tenacity, and spiritual fortitude helped me to achieve my dreams. Before I learned about chanting, I already had the work ethic and I was tenacious, but what I lacked was spiritual fortitude.

I found that as my spiritual fortitude increased, my tenacity also increased, which further boosted my work success. Achieving personal fulfillment, in all areas of my life, started by unlocking the door of my wisdom, my Buddha nature. The three pillars of faith, practice, and study of Buddhism changed everything for the better.

When some people hear the word *faith,* they get turned off because they think of externally imposed rules and obligations. Or they associate faith with a denial of reality. For me, faith is an awareness of your true self, the understanding that the infinite dignity of the universe and the essence of your life are the same. You can be solidly grounded in reality and still recognize the potential for happiness that exists within yourself.

To me, faith is cherishing and developing the potential of one's own precious life.

In this way, I wish for everyone to have faith.

Does this mean I expect everyone to do what I do? Of course not. I just want you to be happy—truly happy.

Reading messages I receive from around the world, I find that many people are seeking new spiritual tools to open their hearts and reveal their inner joy, their Buddha nature. I hope the tools I'm sharing here will do exactly that.

If I can help you to find a clearer way of seeing, or motivate you to fulfill your potential, or in any other way help you become a happier person, then I've succeeded.

However you travel to your higher worlds—whether you choose the same path as me, or another one—I'm cheering for you with my whole heart.

Chapter Four

STAND UP FOR YOUR LIFE

The year was 1255. Mount Fuji's snowcapped summit stood silently in the distance, overlooking Kamakura, the largest city in Japan at the time and the seat of the shogun military government.

Pine trees had dropped a carpet of needles that the wind was collecting into a lush enclave the locals called "Pine Needle Valley." There, in a modest hut, Nichiren picked up his writing brush to create a brief, yet profound, essay titled "On Attaining Buddhahood in This Lifetime."

This is how I imagine the moment when Nichiren created one of my favorite spiritual writings.

He wrote, "When deluded, one is called an ordinary being, but when enlightened, one is called a Buddha. This is similar to a tarnished mirror that will shine like a jewel when polished." He went on to say that chanting Nam-myoho-renge-kyo is the most powerful practice for polishing the mirror of our life.

Mirrors in thirteenth-century Japan were made of shiny metals that would tarnish unless polished regularly. Thus, the analogy of polishing your mirror. We can think of this in modern terms as a mirror covered in dust or grime that we must clean away to see clearly.

When you can see yourself clearly, you can change anything.

I've often described chanting and polishing my life's mirror as "mystical." In the interfaith Beyond Music albums I recorded, we refer to Nam-myoho-renge-kyo as the Mystic Law. And, as mentioned earlier, *myoho* means "Mystic Law."

The "law" here refers to the law of cause and effect. In other words, the Mystic Law is a natural law, like the law of gravity. As we know, you don't need to believe in the law of gravity for it to function and influence you, just as you don't need to believe in the law of cause and effect for it to do the same.

As for its "mystic" aspects, I believe we must experience chanting the Mystic Law to truly understand its deepest significance. I've found that trying to explain the mystical qualities of Nam-myoho-renge-kyo to people who have never tried chanting is like describing the taste of strawberries to someone who has never eaten one.

But I believe everyone can benefit from understanding

the powerful effects of chanting. So, let's look at how chant-ing polishes the mirror of your life.

I'll start by talking a bit about the human mind.

Even before I became interested in Buddhist philosophy, I was fascinated by the power of the subconscious mind. In psychoanalysis, I believe the term is *unconscious mind.* But whenever I hear the word *unconscious,* I can't help thinking of someone who passed out after a wild party. So, I prefer to use the term *subconscious mind.*

Much of what I've found in modern science about the subconscious mind supports ancient Buddhist theories on this subject. These insights are timeless and help explain how the practice of chanting works to improve our karma.

For many years, I've been interested in theories on how the subconscious mind affects our day-to-day behavior and perception of the world. In studying Buddhism, I discovered a parallel construct about layers of perception called "the nine levels of consciousness." (In ancient Buddhist texts, the term meaning "consciousness" also means "perception.")

Our five senses are sight, hearing, smell, taste, and touch. Each one provides us with a level of consciousness. I'll il-lustrate by walking you through another day in my life, my farewell concert in London, on May 3, 2009.

Filled with gratitude for how supportive the UK has always been of my career, I stand onstage, ready to rehearse for the evening show. I gaze out at the vacant seats (sight). I inhale a deep, focused breath (smell). I take a sip of my favorite herbal tea (taste), and I savor the soothing warmth in my throat (touch).

As I put down the cup, I catch the faint scent of sandalwood incense that's burning offstage (smell). I nod to my guitarist, who starts playing the intro of "Proud Mary" (sound).

As I tap my steel-reinforced high heel on the vibrating stage floor (touch), and we get rolling, I run through steps and routines with my dancers (touch). Finally, I look out into the arena again and visualize a packed house, imagining that I'm enveloped in the audience's joyful energy and I'm giving it right back to them.

My sixth level of consciousness is what integrates these five senses into coherent information. In this example, the sixth consciousness is what enabled me to distinguish between an empty arena and my vivid visualization of a packed arena, the same way that you can tell the difference between a picture of food on a restaurant's menu and the food itself.

The seventh level of consciousness is the "thinking mind" and the realm of ego, which is associated with attachment to our lesser self and the life conditions of the lower worlds.

The morning of my rehearsal in London, I'd heard an unpleasant tabloid rumor about me. After my years of chanting and studying Buddhist principles, I'm usually able to shake off such gossip, but for some reason I had to work extra hard to clear my mind before rehearsal so that I could be at my best.

Worrying about what others think of us is an example

of attachment to our lesser self. In my case, worrying about someone's opinion of me temporarily pulled my life condition down.

The seventh level of consciousness is also the level at which our mind can imagine, make plans, and determine the difference between right and wrong. Imagining myself sending love to a huge audience is a seventh-consciousness activity.

This seventh consciousness is what French philosopher René Descartes considered to be proof of his existence when he declared, "I think, therefore I am."

For most of our waking lives, we operate on the level of these seven consciousnesses, taking in sensory data from our first five consciousnesses, automatically processing them with our sixth, and then thinking about all of it with our seventh level.

The eighth level of consciousness is called the *alaya,* where the energy of our karma accumulates. In Sanskrit, *alaya* means "storehouse." Think of the Himalaya mountains— *hima* means "snow," and so *Himalaya* means "the storehouse of snow."

This level of our consciousness receives the results of all our thoughts, words, and deeds—our karma. It's therefore very important and is the main influence on our destiny.

I've come to understand and embrace the idea that everything I experience in life is the karmic result of all my thoughts, words, and deeds—from the lowest lows to the highest highs.

The need for change bulldozed a road
down the center of my mind.
—MAYA ANGELOU

•

Above all, be the heroine of your life,
not the victim.
—NORA EPHRON

•

If you don't like the road you're walking,
start paving another one.
—DOLLY PARTON

Buddhism teaches that everything we experience in life, no matter how minor, is imprinted in this eighth level of our consciousness. Although we may not be able to recall everything with our thinking mind, when the right external stimulus appears, it is possible for any memory from our past to resurface.

The eighth level of consciousness is also the level of what Swiss psychologist Carl Jung called the "collective unconscious," or shared consciousness. All humans share an inborn reservoir of common experience, reaching back to the very beginnings of existence. This is the mystical influence Jung referred to as collective memory (akin to what Buddhists call "collective karma"). It manifests as our instincts and other unseen aspects of our consciousness. This theory of Jung's, that people are intimately connected with both their individual past and the wider past of all humanity, aligns with the Buddhist concept of the eighth consciousness.

Then, at our deepest level, we have the ninth consciousness, known as the *amala,* meaning "pure." This is the shining level of our Buddha nature, our greater self, which cannot be stained by karmic accumulations. This is the transcendent feeling I have when I chant and feel at one with all of life.

This is also the feeling I have when I perform, when I'm transported by the energy of giving and receiving love onstage. One of my favorite moments in my shows was dancing on the metal claw that swept out over the audience. From my perch, I could see individual faces, look into their eyes, experience their joy in the music, and feel a strong connection. I walked off the stage each night overwhelmed by the memory of color, light, sound, and the thousands of smiling faces I saw before me.

Tapping into the *amala* consciousness is the key to transforming our karma. It is pure life force that positively affects all other levels of consciousness for the better.

This root level of our innate Buddhahood and the enlightened essence of the universe—the fundamental reality of life—are one and the same. Nichiren gave expression to this enlightened essence as Nam-myoho-renge-kyo and described our bodies as "the palace of the ninth consciousness."

By chanting Nam-myoho-renge-kyo, we swing open the gates to this majestic palace of enlightenment.

Manifesting the life condition of Buddhahood, here and now, as you are, is standing up for your life—opening the wellspring of wisdom, courage, and compassion within your essence, enabling you to overcome any adversity.

I like to imagine the layers of consciousness as a water fountain. The ninth consciousness is your very own deep reservoir of pure water. Chanting is opening a pipeline to bring that clean water rushing up through your other layers of consciousness, to purify and clarify your perception of the world.

Accessing this purifying force is crucial, since the influence of karma is often less about what happens in life and more about how we perceive what happens in life—how our internal "sediment" clouds our view of the world.

This thought is reflected in valuable guidance I once received at an SGI chanting meeting:

When we are upset, it's easy to blame others. The root of our feelings, however, is within us. For example, imagine yourself as a glass of water. Now, imagine past negative experiences as sediment at the bottom of your glass. Next, think of an unpleasant situation or person as a spoon. When the spoon stirs, the sediment clouds your water. It may appear that the spoon caused the water to cloud—but without sediment, the water would remain clear. Even if we remove the spoon, our sediment still remains—lying in wait for the next spoon to appear. On the other hand, if we remove our sediment, no matter what happens, no matter how a spoon stirs, our water will remain clear.

Whenever I remind myself of this simple analogy, I feel relief at the knowledge that I have control over my life condition, which colors any thoughts that come into my consciousness, as well as my responses to any negativity that may arise. I know I can remove any sediment in the "water glass of my life," so to speak, by tapping into my Buddhahood.

From this vantage point, it is easy to see the value of connecting to your deepest level of consciousness, the pure spring water of your soul. When you do so, you can speed the transformation of your destiny by increasing the flow of wisdom and decreasing new actions that could pollute your water.

This optimistic, empowering view reminds us that both positive and negative karma exist in our deep consciousness. Remember that abundant goodness, all of the positive causes we've made (in thought, word, and deed), are also recorded in our storehouse of karma. When we are mindful of this, it serves as a great inspiration to create more good karma each day, in every step we take.

Whether you believe that your deepest levels of consciousness span only this lifetime or encompass many others, I'm sure that you've had times when an unexpected thought, a hunch, or a feeling pops into your mind that you can't explain. I certainly have. Sometimes, the hunch holds the answer to a dilemma you're facing, or tells you which choice to make. If you're like me, you probably thought, *Where did that come from?*

These flashes of intuition or instinct rise up from our eighth consciousness.

I first experienced this kind of helpful internal guidance system as a little girl. Running around the backwoods of Nutbush, whenever I sensed danger, like the first time I came across a snake in the grass, a deep awareness told me to run fast and far. No one taught me to do that—I was driven by instinct.

I used to marvel at the amazing ingenuity of animals in the countryside. I saw young birds that had never built a nest listen to their instincts—the collective wisdom of Mother Nature—to solve challenges they'd never faced. What I realize now is that animals solve problems by listening to their inherent wisdom, the awareness arising from their eighth consciousness. They allow themselves to feel the energy flowing all around them.

That's what I try to do in my life, and listening to my inner voice serves me well. Two of my dancers, the twin sisters Karen and Sharon Owens, told me more than once that I seemed to sense things that were happening behind me onstage during a performance. They noticed that I would turn around exactly when someone had missed a step, or when one of the guys in the band was goofing off. "How did you know?" they'd ask.

Honestly, I'm not sure, but when I sensed something out of sync on my stage, I'd dance over with a smile and send some love to my team to keep everyone feeling strong and focused. The twins told me I must have eyes in the back of my head, and we'd laugh about it. Really, I was just listening to my inner voice and tuning in to the energy around me. I think we can all do this if we focus on tuning in to ourselves.

Where does that "tuning in" come from?

We know that DNA passes on physical characteristics from generation to generation. I trust that science will eventually prove our invisible attributes are also passed down through generations—that the spiritual aspects of our karma are held in what I view as our spiritual DNA.

A bird is a bird because of its physical DNA, but a bird's

ability to accomplish tasks it has never been taught comes from its spiritual DNA. This is part of the greater, unseen energy and wisdom that flow through all life.

I believe we all share the same inner wisdom that we find in Mother Nature. That's the voice of our Buddha wisdom, or Christ consciousness, deep within us.

It's simply a matter of cutting through the noise of our ego so we can receive these messages. When we can see past the distractions and perceive our minds clearly, our inner wisdom will guide us to take the best actions at any given moment.

When you can see yourself clearly, the path will also become clear, and you will have the power to change whatever stands in the way of your success, health, and happiness.

Still, the functions of the mind are truly mysterious, and it's hard to determine where the "thinking self" exists. Often, it appears that thoughts come from nowhere, yet they create the reality of the world in which we live.

Everything humanity has ever created began with a thought.

Our thoughts lead to our words and deeds, which create our karma. Marcus Aurelius, the Roman emperor and philosopher, alluded to this when he said, "The happiness of your life depends upon the quality of your thoughts."

That's the reason I try to infuse cheerfulness and humor into my thoughts, and ultimately my words, to help brighten my day. Friends have pointed out to me that even when I talk with them about some of the painful things that happened in my past, I do so with humor.

You know what they say about comedy, right? It's tragedy, plus time.

I'm glad that I've gotten to a place where I can laugh about my life, and about myself; it lightens up my thoughts. This is important, because our thoughts and the way we think direct every area of our lives.

When was the last time you considered how thoughts arise?

When I had a stroke in late 2013, I was sharply reminded of the importance of our brain functions, and the way we generate thoughts. As my incredible medical team worked on my recovery, I also went to work to help myself heal. I wanted to understand the functions of my brain so I could envision my path back to wholeness.

Here's what I discovered:

Science tells us there is a level of communication going on among the neurons within our brains. Neurons are those lively, specialized nerve cells that transmit information in our bodies and facilitate our ability to think. In fact, the neurons in your brain are enabling you to absorb the information I'm sharing with you here.

Neurons communicate with one another through rapid electrical impulses, which create brain waves. Sensors can detect these waves, revealing a continuous spectrum of consciousness that ranges from slow-vibrating waves with low frequency to fast-vibrating waves with high frequency.

When we're in deep sleep, our brains produce waves with very low frequency, and while we're actively thinking, our brains produce waves with much higher frequency. These brain waves are measured in hertz (Hz)—a unit of frequency equal to one cycle per second. In sleep, the lowest ranges are under 4Hz, and for highly concentrated thinking, the highest are at 40Hz or more.

The brain is truly an amazing organic machine!

Studies have shown that rhythmic chanting can bring our brain waves into a vibrational frequency between 7Hz and 8Hz. This is also the typical frequency of brain waves when we are creatively visualizing, making music and art, and experiencing other calm, creative modes of thinking.

I find it interesting that the vibration of our brain waves while we are chanting also corresponds with what is known as Earth's fundamental frequency of 7.83Hz. This is called the base Schumann resonance, after physicist Winfried Schumann, who predicted it. Perhaps such similarities are only a "coincidence." But since I don't believe in coincidence, I expect that someday we will discover a meaningful significance behind this vibrational alignment.

In the meantime, I'm delighted that there is already scientific evidence of the physical and emotional benefits of chanting. Thousands of years ago, Buddhists began using the tool of chanting to help with a variety of mental ailments. Today in modern psychiatry, doctors are increasingly acknowledging the positive effects of chanting on mental health challenges, including self-esteem issues, addiction rehabilitation, and post-traumatic stress recovery.

After experiencing the benefits of this practice for nearly five decades, I believe that there will be a time when Buddhism will be viewed as the science of spirit, and regarded as good medicine for both the mind and the body.

Over the past decade, as I faced so many obstacles with my health—first the stroke, then intestinal cancer, kidney failure, and more—the cumulative effect of many years of spiritual practice was invaluable. I was never shaken, at least not for long, by any health issue that arose. I mustered all my resilience. And I know that my ability to smoothly navigate the healing process came from my spiritual training.

Throughout many hospital visits and multiple surgeries, I kept this empowering message in mind from Nichiren:

> *Nam-myoho-renge-kyo is like the roar of a lion.*
> *What illness can therefore be an obstacle?*

Remembering this call to courage, I summoned my inner lion and roared.

I roared and roared, and kept on roaring until I overcame every health challenge, just like I'd overcome every challenge that came before.

It's not the load that breaks you down,
it's the way you carry it.
—LENA HORNE

•

Difficulties are not necessarily unfortunate.
It depends on your attitude.
You can either let difficulties crush you,
or you can use them to build your strength.
—INDIRA GANDHI

•

I have stood on a mountain of no's for one yes.
—B. SMITH

The challenges we face in life can come from outside ourselves, or they can come from within.

I know from personal experience that there are sometimes negative voices in your head, and they can be dangerous. These voices may say you're too old, too young, too gay, too straight, too thin, too fat, too this, too that. The voices may tell you it's too late for your dreams, or that no one will love you. They may tell you all sorts of lies to keep you trapped in unhealthy cycles of self-doubt.

Maybe you've allowed your negative voices to undermine your self-esteem, to hinder your work, or to keep you locked in unhealthy relationships. If so, it's time to tell those voices you've heard their propaganda, and you're not going to take it anymore. Dismiss them, and you will be the only one holding the pen as you write the story of your life.

I know all about taking back power from negative voices.

When I was a child, my mind was imprinted with the sound of my parents bickering. That was replaced by the emotional abuse of my first marriage. There were many times in my life when negative voices reverberated inside my head. I surrendered to these negative voices when I tried to kill myself during my darkest days. But the fact that I survived made me realize I had a purpose—a mission.

I decided to stand up for my life and fight for my future.

Standing up meant that I had to start by sitting down and searching within. The most effective fight for my future had to begin inside my own mind.

I explored my subconscious mind and tapped into my Buddhahood. I flooded every level of my consciousness with the pure water of my chanting prayers and, through my spiritual practice, I slowly but surely quieted the negative voices until they were silenced.

After I learned about the nine consciousnesses, I came to see such negative voices as karmic residue—that sediment we were talking about before—rising up from the eighth level to torment my mind.

Another way to help resolve such voices is to think of them as ghosts of past experiences that are appearing in the present. Perhaps you've heard negative voices echoing in your head from your past. I think everyone deals with ghost voices at one time or another.

Dispel them once and for all.

It doesn't really matter whether you know the exact origin of these negative mental messages. What matters is getting rid of them. When you allow them to linger, the toxic internal dialogue intensifies, which creates fear—internalized fear—that sabotages your decision-making.

When you make decisions based on fear, whether consciously or subconsciously, you end up attracting exactly what you were trying to avoid. This is why it is crucial to control your mind and allow your decisions to flow from a place of authenticity based on your happiness rather than on your fear.

I hope you never again hear negative voices in your head.

If you do, however, here's my simple advice to exorcise them: Stop believing them. Silence the ghost voices and the negativity they spread by rejecting their poisonous stories. See them for what they truly are—remnants of the past, something that doesn't exist. They are illusions and delusions.

If you fall into the trap of believing such voices, then you're holding on to the past. Internal negativity is always rooted in the past. And holding on to the past only stands in the way of your future.

Cherished memories of good times you've had with loved ones, your past accomplishments, victorious memories of overcoming adversity, favorite songs and movies from yesteryear—these are examples of positive things that can add value to the present. But that's not the same as holding on to, or reliving, the past, which can be very unhealthy, especially if you're recycling unpleasant experiences.

One thing I know for sure: We must learn the lessons from any unpleasant experiences we've had. If we do not, they will continue to hold power over us, and we will feel compelled to repeat them.

Holding on to the past also causes an inaccurate perception of the present, which can cause suffering. Perceiving ourselves, others, and the world we occupy clearly, as they really are, is the only path to happiness. And clear perception is always grounded in the present.

Step out of the history that is holding you back.
Step into the new story
you are willing to create.
—OPRAH WINFREY

•

Can't nothin' make your life work
if you ain't the architect.
—TERRY McMILLAN, *DISAPPEARING ACTS*

•

I choose to make the rest of my life
the best of my life.
—LOUISE HAY

Perception is powerful, and how we view ourselves is entwined with how others see us. I've experienced this first-hand. Since my twenties, some people close to me have told me I'm an intelligent, talented, strong, beautiful woman. I was happy to hear all these adjectives, but, privately, I never felt beautiful.

Most kids are self-conscious about their own appearance and begin noticing other people's appearances more intensely as they grow up, especially as they become teenagers. That was definitely the case with me.

I never felt that I fit the mold of what a "pretty girl" was supposed to look like. I was skinny—in my eyes, much too skinny to be considered beautiful. In those days, being curvy was the ideal, and that wasn't me.

When I played basketball in high school, I'd often spend the night at my friend Carolyn's house before important games. Sometimes, when I'd forget to bring a change of clothes, I'd borrow hers. Her jeans made my legs look bigger, and that made me so happy. *Someday,* I swore to her, and to myself, *someday I will have long hair and big hips and legs that everyone will think are beautiful.*

It's funny looking back on that now because even though my wish came true, and even though I eventually became nearly as famous for my legs as for my talent, I still couldn't see my own beauty.

When I first became a performer, I'd spend so much time getting ready for shows, trying to make sure every hair was in place and my outfit was perfect. Yet, when I looked in the mirror, I still heard voices telling me I wasn't ever going to look as good as I hoped.

When I was growing up, my parents only rarely expressed praise or affection to me. Looking back, I can see that they were so busy disliking each other, and themselves, that they didn't have enough love to share with anyone else. In the famous words of RuPaul, "If you can't love yourself, how in the hell you gonna love somebody else?"

Amen.

At the time, though, I thought there was something wrong with me, that maybe I was unlovable. I cannot recall ever being told I was beautiful as a child. I remember watching my mother delicately care for my sister's hair as I waited patiently for my turn. In my heart, I secretly wished that she'd caress my face and comb my hair in the caring way she did for my sister, but I was always disappointed. Her roughness when she combed my hair told me what she felt for me, or, what she didn't feel for me.

A child who feels unloved grows up to feel unwanted and unattractive.

Despite my best efforts to rise above the dysfunction of my childhood, it naturally seeped into my consciousness. I tried to move away from the negativity of that period, but ghost voices stayed with me. All through my twenties and early thirties, the ghost voices told me a lot of lies.

I'd hear critics in the media saying something about me

that they may not have thought sounded bad, but to me their words were a reiteration of how unattractive I was. Adjectives like "raunchy," "wild," and "gritty" reinforced what the negative voices in the back of my head were saying: *Tina, you're not pretty.*

Nothing I did seemed to change this pattern, and it didn't help that I was in an abusive environment. Even after I stood up for my life and broke free, I still couldn't bring myself to see my own beauty. And when I say beauty, I also mean value.

Then, after several years of chanting, I had an epiphany. I realized that I had internalized all that past negativity, starting from childhood, and was still carrying it around, which pulled down my life condition.

This may seem obvious now, looking back on my (well-publicized) life, but at the time it was a startling revelation.

Then and there, I made a vow to stop believing the old negativity and replace unhealthy thoughts with healthy ones. If a negative thought arose, I'd repeat a positive one eight times in a row to counteract it. Soon, I began loving myself, imperfections and all. I stopped comparing myself to others (never compare yourself to others), and at last I started to look good to myself.

The beauty standards of others made no difference to me—the only thing that mattered was how I felt about myself. I still thought I had a masculine form with legs like a pony. But I finally began to truly love my form, my legs, and apparently it showed.

After this transformation of consciousness, I was invited to perform at a high-profile event shortly before my breakthrough album *Private Dancer* was released. I did my own hair and makeup and chose clothing from my own closet, something I'd be comfortable wearing rather than what I thought would impress others.

The press comments about me that evening were filled with adjectives I'd never seen used to describe me. They were the same positive words I had started telling myself when I looked in the mirror; words I wished I'd heard from my mother—"beautiful," "magnetic," and "radiant."

The deep changes in my consciousness and perception had not only caused a transformation in me, but had also affected the people around me. They saw me differently because I was different. I radiated self-acceptance and confidence.

Replacing delusions with clarity, replacing negative messages with positive ones, is the way we can free ourselves from suffering.

If there is any part of yourself that you aren't valuing, loving, and honoring, I hope you will use the positive influences you have available—chanting, meditation, yoga, exercise, affirmations, psychotherapy—to cleanse your mind of negativity, past and present, and transform those poisons into something of value (more on this in chapter five).

Who among us has not at some point in time
succumbed to the propaganda, looked in a mirror,
and felt ourselves to be wanting?
—MARCIA ANN GILLESPIE

•

The kind of beauty I want most
is the hard-to-get kind that comes from within:
strength, courage, dignity.
—RUBY DEE

•

Not everything that is faced can be changed;
but nothing can be changed until it is faced.
—JAMES BALDWIN

Even when we are successful at silencing internal sources of negativity, we will still face negativity from sources outside ourselves, such as the scourge of discrimination.

When I was young, not much was expected of women, especially a "colored woman" like me. Racial discrimination was legal for the first quarter-century of my life. Those laws may have changed, but people are not as quick to evolve.

I thought that the best career I could aspire to was to be a teacher or a nurse. I was always good with younger children, and so my mother also figured I'd become a pediatric nurse or a teacher, nurse being her preference because it paid better. I did work as a nurse's assistant and learned a lot from the experience. But in my heart of hearts, I always felt I would teach someday.

At last, with this book, which I see as a form of teaching, I'm fulfilling that long-held dream—and in my eighties, no less. I hope this fact alone will inspire you to never give up on your dreams.

When I was traveling around the country with the Ike & Tina Turner Revue in the early 1960s, there were white hotels and colored hotels. And believe it or not, sometimes even the colored hotels wouldn't let us in, because performers were looked down upon by some Black hotel owners. So, I learned about discrimination even within the Black community.

Racism and classism were just the start of my experiences with prejudice. Later, I faced ageism and sexism, too. When

I was forty-two, I was trying to restart my career. As a Black single mother who was staying at friends' homes because I couldn't afford my own place after my divorce, I had to break through multiple barriers to achieve my career goals, and sometimes they seemed insurmountable.

Show business, despite its reputation for being liberal, was pretty repressive when I was looking for work as a solo artist. I hit up against big biases, with some executives saying I was too old (at only forty-two!). And my being female and Black didn't fit their preconceived notions of what a rock 'n' roll star should look like.

But I didn't let anything get me down as I continued to stand up for my life. I persevered with patience, compassion, and a "never give up" attitude. I understood that I was not only changing my own karma, but in light of the eighth and ninth levels of consciousness, I was also helping to change the collective karma of society and our whole human family.

My wish is that, in some way, my personal history of breaking barriers has resonated into the world and helped other people—including you—to advance toward happiness and an awareness of your beautiful Buddha consciousness.

After nearly half a century of tapping the deepest levels of consciousness through spiritual practice, I sincerely believe that you can change anything for good by weaving an awareness of your inherent Buddha nature into the fabric of your daily life.

Whether you're first learning about Buddhist philosophy, you're a longtime chanter, or even if you never want to hear another word about chanting after reading this book, please keep this sentiment with you—my personal interpretation of the pure ninth consciousness of Buddhahood:

I believe we each hold within us what I call a "coin of God," a piece of the eternal energy of the universe, the essence of Buddha nature. A coin is a minted piece of value from the greater system to which it belongs, and each living being is a priceless treasure piece, molded from our greater universe. May we each cherish ourselves and extend this kindness to all living beings with whom we share this blessed planet.

Chapter Five

CHANGING POISON
INTO MEDICINE

Gemstones of varying sizes and colors gleamed in the midday heat, swaying gracefully on gold and silver stems as far as the eye could see. I made my way through this surreal treasure field, plucking gems and filling the burlap sack on my shoulder with my sparkling collection. *Better take it in before it's too heavy to lift,* I thought, as a voice startled me back to reality.

"Anna Mae, you can carry more than that," said a field manager.

Daydreaming again, I had transported myself to a place of wonder, while in fact I was toiling in a cotton field alongside my elementary school classmates.

Summer vacation was my favorite time. However, because

I was a Black child, my school break was much shorter than that of white students. The Black kids all went to "colored schools" in those days, and we were expected to help the adults working in the fields during cotton-picking season. Our summer vacation ended in July, when we'd start school, then we'd be let out for picking season from mid-September until November.

Though my summer breaks were short, they were a welcome time for me because I could stay outside.

One of my favorite pastimes was searching for lucky four-leaf clovers. Whenever I discovered one, I promptly brushed it off and swallowed it. In some way, I hoped that eating them could help me change my luck. I didn't realize that my luck—my destiny—was already inside me.

With all that I experienced from those early days through my move to St. Louis in my late teens, then becoming "Tina Turner," giving birth to my beautiful sons and raising them, and achieving a level of stardom, I came to see that every life has its share of problems.

I've never met anyone who didn't have problems of one sort or another. If we find ourselves without any problems, it's just a matter of time until something pops up.

That's life!

Don't worry if you think you're the only one facing challenges.

If the people around you don't seem to have problems, that just means you don't know them well enough to see their troubles, or they're very good at hiding them. Problems are inescapable for all living beings. As Nichiren said: "No one can avoid problems, not even sages."

Living a joyful life, I've found, is not about trying to avoid the unavoidable. Joy comes from summoning a strong life force to overcome problems, from the smallest irritation to the biggest disaster.

You may have been born with a natural enthusiasm for facing your problems. I sure wasn't.

Though I didn't run away from problems, I also didn't really see the point of facing them. Whatever difficulties came my way, my motto was simply: "I'll go on." Somehow, I found the will to keep going, but I didn't face what was holding me back.

It wasn't until I experienced life-threatening difficulties and turned my attention inward that I discovered the life-altering Buddhist concept of *changing poison into medicine*.

This concept filled my thoughts as I stood onstage at London's historic Aldwych Theatre in April 2018, gazing out at the red velvet seats and gorgeous walls adorned with gilded plasterwork.

It was opening night of *Tina: The Tina Turner Musical,* and I wanted to have a quiet moment in the hall before our guests took their seats for the show. Looking through the eyes of that little girl in the cotton fields who dreamed of one day being surrounded by grace and beauty, I felt proud of her, of me, for never giving up our dreams.

The reward is not so great
without the struggle.
—WILMA RUDOLPH

•

There are two rules in life.
Number one: Never give up.
Number two: Never forget rule number one.
—DUKE ELLINGTON

•

What really matters is not whether we have problems
but how we go through them.
—ROSA PARKS

I still get chills thinking about the show's opening scene, which depicts me as a child in the fields, and the many poisons I had to change during my journey from the past to where I was now. I got chills again later that night when I joined the cast for the curtain call and looked into the cheering, smiling, tear-streaked faces in the audience.

If you find inspiration in my life, then I hope you will remember that you are equally capable of changing poison into medicine in your life, too.

Let's look at what exactly "changing poison into medicine" means.

This phrase originated with a wise man named Nagarjuna, a Buddhist scholar who lived in India around the year 200 A.D. He likened the wisdom of the Lotus Sutra to "a great physician who can change poison into medicine."

In Japan a thousand years later, Nichiren quoted this phrase when he taught his disciples about facing problems and using them to increase wisdom, courage, and compassion.

When problems arise, it's common for our feelings to sink and our life condition to dip into the lower worlds, which often makes matters worse. Whether conscious of it or not, if we are operating from a place in the lower worlds, even our best efforts to solve problems can have the opposite effect.

Pressure builds, old habits surface, feelings about similar problems arise, and ghost voices in our heads offer bad advice, or our ego tries to take over.

Have you ever noticed how the ego loves problems? It's a

chance for the ego to tell you, and everyone else, how right it is (or perhaps how misunderstood it is). If you've ever allowed your ego to get involved in solving problems, you know that can make a bad situation worse.

Yet, until my early thirties, this was how I responded to problems. Both the problems and my responses to them were like poisons. When I couldn't see myself or my life clearly, my distorted perception caused me to respond to adversity in ways that compromised my good intentions, leading me into even more negative cycles of behavior.

However, when I began attending SGI chanting meetings at my friend Ana Shorter's home, I heard people share stories about using problems to elevate their lives to an even happier condition than before their problems arose. They said they had "changed poison into medicine" and promised that I could do the same.

I was happy for them, but I couldn't imagine how my problems could be of value to me. Though I desperately wanted to believe it was possible to transform problems into benefits, I had a hard time seeing how my woes could do anything but cause further trouble.

Among the members of our chanting group were a few older Japanese ladies who glowed with a peaceful air of joy and compassion. They had lived through the horrors of World War II, and one had survived the atomic bombing of Nagasaki. They had moved to the United States with their military husbands.

After chanting with them one day, our conversation turned to my problems. Kimiko, one of the ladies, asked me, "Tina, you say you have too many problems to list. What sort of problems do you mean?"

I don't wear my heart on my sleeve, but something about the high life condition of these women opened me up, and I confided in them. I wasn't complaining, just stating the facts about my situation.

Leaving—and divorcing—Ike proved to be more complicated than I had ever imagined. I was facing an army of lawyers filing lawsuits against me for walking out on concert and recording contracts I was supposed to do with Ike. Meanwhile, I was also being harassed by thugs Ike sent to intimidate me, whose tactics included setting fire to one of my friend's cars and firing bullets through my windows.

On top of that, I was in debt, I had no savings, no income, no place of my own to live (my sons and I were staying with Ana and Wayne Shorter), and I was a Black woman in my forties trying to restart my career as a solo rock 'n' roll artist in an industry that prizes young white males above all else. Plus I was in need of new management. Oh, and I had health challenges, too.

As I was wrapping up my sad monologue, my fellow chanters' faces lit up with smiles. To my surprise, they looked as if they were impressed, perhaps even wonderstruck.

Everyone clapped with real enthusiasm, cheering: "Congratulations, Tina! You are so fortunate!"

Pardon me?

It sounded like they said, "Congratulations."

For a moment, I thought that they didn't understand anything I had just said, or maybe I had misheard them.

No, I heard them right—they were congratulating me.

"Why in the world would you congratulate me for this mess?" I asked.

And that's when I really began to understand the principle of changing poison into medicine.

"When you raise your life condition," Kimiko said, "you are capable of transforming all the negative energy in those unfortunate situations into the opposite, positive energy of good fortune.

"As bad as it is," she reassured me, "it can become the same level of good, or even better.

"Since you have so many major problems," Kimiko continued, "that means you have the opportunity to create even more positives by changing poison into medicine. That's why we congratulate you."

I was so relieved and excited to hear this. I went from seeing a pile of negatives to recognizing a treasure trove. If problems could really be used as fuel to propel my life upward, then I figured I was set to become America's first woman in space. I felt like I had enough fuel at that point to go interstellar.

As intensely bad as the problems are, that's how intensely good the benefits can be, I repeated to myself.

Difficulties, opposition, criticism—these things
are meant to be overcome, and there is a certain joy
in facing them and coming out on top.
—VIJAYA LAKSHMI PANDIT

Take your broken heart, make it into art.
—CARRIE FISHER

Character cannot be developed in ease and quiet.
Only through experience of trial
and suffering can the soul be strengthened,
ambition inspired, and success achieved.
—HELEN KELLER

The concept of changing poison into medicine is based on the idea that when you raise your life condition, you can use the resulting wisdom, courage, and compassion to convert any negative into a positive. If you have a minor problem, you can transform it into a minor benefit. If you have a major problem, it has the potential to become a major benefit.

Changing poison into medicine, then, starts with the simple step of facing your problems with the confidence that you have the power within you not just to overcome challenges, but also to thrive *because* of them—to rise up to greater heights than you ever have before.

The key is raising our life condition, as we explored in chapter two. When you lack confidence, when you've lost focus, or when your mind-set needs a boost, then supercharge your intention by chanting, meditating, exercising, or whatever wholesome practice lifts you up.

Elevating your life condition is essential to creating meaningful, lasting changes in your life.

Only when we achieve a high life condition can we face any circumstance head-on with an open, embracing spirit. There is then no problem too difficult to overcome, no obstacle too stubborn to move.

From this elevated state, we can see that the obstacles we face hold the lessons we must learn to make our dreams come true.

With this understanding, we can call up the wisdom to choose positive responses and actions (in thought, word, and deed) that will lead to constructive changes and help us to avoid making situations worse for ourselves, or others.

Thanks to this process, I began to see that any problems in my life were also opportunities for growth and becoming a better, happier version of myself. Every obstacle could help me to become a wiser, stronger, and more compassionate person.

Like the lotus, the deeper and thicker the mud I was mired in, the more beautifully my flower could bloom. Not despite the mud, but *because* of it.

I also saw the truth of the old saying that when you point your finger, three of your fingers point back at you—a reminder to always check ourselves.

In the Buddhist community, we say, "There is no guilt, only responsibility."

This means that when a problem arises, we shouldn't view it as something we deserve because of our negative karma. Nor should we dwell on who's to blame. Blame is the realm of ego.

Instead, we must take responsibility for our actions and handle problems calmly and rationally, aiming to create greater happiness for ourselves and everyone involved. This is sometimes easier said than done, whether it's a major or minor life problem, or an "Operation Oops," as I call the funnier, *I Love Lucy* mishaps we experience. I've had my share of "Operation Oops," like the night I had a little too much fun with my band at the close of one of our tours.

It was the night before our last show in New Zealand, and we had a party where the entire band (all men, except for my backup dancers) surprised me by dressing up in women's clothes to look like me (not even close!) and lip-synced my songs. They told me it was my turn to be sung to, and I loved every minute of it.

I had three or four glasses of champagne, no big deal for most people, but since I'm not a drinker, it wiped me out. Then, I stayed up much later than I usually do the night before a show, and on top of that, something I ate did a number on my stomach.

The next day, I felt the full force of food poisoning, fatigue, and a headache. I could barely drag myself from my hotel bed most of the day, let alone imagine performing. Worse still, this last show was on an outdoor stage, and as the Kiwis would say, it was pissing down rain.

But there was no question of my canceling that show. I had survived far worse in my life than food poisoning and a headache. My fans had paid to see me perform, made sacrifices to get tickets, traveled to the venue, and were willing to stand in the rain without shelter. So, I set out to change the poison into medicine. I chanted to muster my strength and give my audience a performance beyond their expectations.

About an hour into chanting, I felt the nausea and pain leaving my body. I was energized, calm, and vibrating with anticipation, eager to get to the stage for the sound check and to give the performance of my life.

When I arrived at the venue, the rain was pouring, the stage was slippery, and the wind was intense. Timmy Cappello, my sax player, was wearing his big Doc Martens boots and was gingerly making his way across the stage. Meanwhile, I was in my high-heel Louboutins. Not only was I expected to walk in them, I had to dance!

When it was time for the show to begin, I sang and danced my heart out. I even left the stage tent to get soaking wet with my fans. I had an absolute blast. Chanting, and solid faith that I could transform the problem into something better than expected, had turned poison into medicine yet again.

As I mentioned earlier, the ego loves problems. While I was lying in bed feeling sick in New Zealand, my ego was chiming in, whispering for me to forget about that show, listing all the problems I'd face. I knew better than to listen, and quickly flipped it around.

The ego relishes problems, not because it wants to change them into positives, but because the ego can use trouble to keep us under its spell. It veils itself in problems to perpetuate drama, take the easy way out, avoid responsibility, and reiterate its superiority over others.

Sometimes our ego would have us believe that we are perfect just as we are, that we don't need others to teach us anything.

Even when we have our ego in check, if we have no one to help guide us in life, it's hard to have a true perspective on where we stand, or where we wish to go. It can be a challenge to know how to make positive changes without an example to encourage us and light our way.

Buddhist tradition teaches that one of the keys to breaking free from the binds of ego is to seek out a mentor who can help us raise our life condition. Mentorship cracks apart the lesser self of ego and opens up the higher self of Buddha nature.

If you've apprenticed a trade, or if you're an artist or athlete, you probably know something about the mentor-disciple dynamic. Yet, these days, it seems that the time-tested bonds of the mentor-disciple relationship have weakened. The notion that you can somehow learn everything you need to know on your own has become common.

If you're not certain of the value of mentorship, think of how many elite athletes or professional sports teams train without a coach. Zero. How many of your favorite films are made without a producer or director? Zero. How many of the best schools in the world function without teachers? Zero.

It's safe to say that every great leader, in any field, first had a great mentor.

Finding a mentor who inspires and guides your growth is a life-changing experience. Mentors help us to transcend the limits, or perceived limits, of our abilities. A mentor can be anyone who teaches us and helps us to grow in ways we couldn't have on our own.

Here I am in the late 1970s, reading about the principle of "changing poison into medicine," which helped me transform my life.

A happy moment captured from my "day in the life" story in chapter two, having a blast with Cher on her 1977 television show.

I'm proud mother Tina, sharing a laugh with my beloved sons Craig (left) and Ronnie (right) at home in Los Angeles in 1979.

Relaxing in my personalized director's chair from the film *Tommy*, with part of my cherished book collection adorning our den wall.

Polishing my life by reciting the Lotus Sutra and chanting
Nam-myoho-renge-kyo during my morning prayers.

Striking my best Wonder Woman power pose and feeling rainbow high as my solo career begins to take flight in the early 1980s.

8

I sang my heart out for the SGI Buddhist peace festival in Washington, D.C., 1982, where I vowed to always inspire hope through my music.

9

Chanting with appreciation in New York City the weekend that my film *Mad Max Beyond Thunderdome* became a 1985 summer box office hit.

10

Feeling emotional and honored as I receive the
Essence Award in 1993 after my dear friend
Ann-Margret surprised me with an onstage tribute.

11

Giving hugs at St. Jude Children's Research Hospital, which
I proudly support, in my home state of Tennessee in 2000.

12

Gazing out the window of my second-floor
chanting room, I soak in the beautiful sight of
my wedding guests arriving in July 2013.

13

My delight was clear to see as I returned to
the Beyond studio in 2017 during a welcome
interlude between medical treatments.

I always love strolling through the garden before my evening prayers as the sun sets over Lake Zürich.

No matter what accomplishments you achieve,
somebody helped you.
—ALTHEA GIBSON

•

A mentor is someone who allows you to see
the higher part of yourself when sometimes
it becomes hidden to your own view.
—OPRAH WINFREY

•

Show me a successful individual
and I'll show you someone who had positive
influences in his or her life.... A mentor.
—DENZEL WASHINGTON

Mentors also help us see ourselves in ways we can't on our own. At any age, we can find a mentor in life. If we don't have access to a mentor in person, we can experience the wisdom of a mentor through the written word.

Looking back, I've been fortunate to have a number of mentors in my life. My first mentor was my cousin Margaret, who taught me about the birds and the bees, and how to take care of myself. During my teen years, I was fortunate to have some great teachers in high school, and I also had the Hendersons, the family I worked for. They compassionately taught me manners and how to conduct myself in society. They also showed me how a healthy relationship should work, and provided me with an example of higher life conditions to aspire to.

Although my first marriage was famously a catastrophe, there were some positives in the beginning. I was only a teenager when I met Ike, and I didn't know anything about the music business. At first, when we were friends, he was my musical mentor, teaching me about the entertainment industry, recording techniques, and performance styles. That mentorship was short-lived, however, and ended by the time we got married.

Later, I was fortunate to meet my spiritual mentor, Daisaku Ikeda, the world's leading voice of Nichiren Buddhist philosophy, who gave me words of wisdom that changed my life.

I am thankful that I encountered my manager, Roger

Davies, who became my greatest career mentor and guided me to a number one record and the worldwide success I'd always dreamed about.

And then, I met Erwin Bach, my mentor in true love, my unwavering life partner, my soul mate and husband. Being with Erwin has taught me to love without giving up who I am, as we grant each other the freedom and space to be individuals at the same time we are a couple. Erwin, who is a force of nature in his own right, has never been the least bit intimidated by my career, my talents, or my fame. He shows me that true love doesn't require the dimming of my light so that he can shine. On the contrary, we are the light of each other's lives, and we want to shine as bright as we can, together.

From my youth, I was somehow blessed with an instinct to seek out people who know more than I do, and to learn from them to help improve myself. That's the essence of any mentorship.

Maybe we all have the instinct to seek out a mentor, but modern society has suppressed this feeling, with its increasingly antisocial social media and emphasis on individualism bordering on isolationism. Hopefully, this trend will reverse, and the value of seeking knowledge from those who know more than we do will be prized again.

In 2014, my friend Herbie Hancock was invited to give the prestigious Norton Lectures at Harvard University, where he shared great insights on the topics of mentorship and changing poison into medicine. Herbie related lessons from his jazz mentor, Miles Davis, who taught him that "a great mentor can provide a path to finding your own true answers," and to always "reach up while reaching down; grow while helping others."

Jazz music itself is an example of changing poison into medicine.

African Americans created jazz, a great medicine for people's hearts, out of the poisonous experience of slavery. Jazz developed from African culture, gospel music, and blues to lift up the spirits of oppressed people, and now it brings joy to people the world over.

Jazz holds a special place in my heart, too.

When I left Ike in 1976, I was penniless. I wanted to work, but it was difficult to relaunch as a solo act. Whenever someone heard the name "Tina," they'd say, "Where's Ike?" I lacked the most basic resources I needed to start my new life. Through those hardest times, two jazz musicians and their families helped to keep me and my sons afloat. As I mentioned earlier, Wayne Shorter and his family chanted with us and took us in when we had nowhere to go, and Herbie Hancock and his wife, Gigi, also attended chanting meetings with me.

They inspired me to never give up, to dream even bigger dreams.

Years later, in 1982, Wayne, Herbie, and I had the honor of performing at a Buddhist peace festival in Washington,

D.C. At that event, we vowed to be musical Bodhisattvas: to create value in society by inspiring hope and peace through our artistic careers. A quarter of a century later, we reunited to perform together—this time on Herbie's jazz album *River: The Joni Letters,* for which we shared the Grammy Award for Album of the Year.

I'm happy to say that I've won more Grammys than I can hold, but this was the only time I've received the Album of the Year award, and to share it with old friends was even sweeter. To me, it was the result of each of us changing poison into medicine repeatedly throughout the years, because of our musical Bodhisattva vow. What a joyful way to come full circle with my jazz friends.

"What do you want in life, Tina?" I recall Wayne asking me one day.

He had returned home from a jazz tour the week after the Fourth of July in 1976 and found me scrubbing his kitchen floor. He and Ana tried to get me to stop doing things like this around the house during the five months that I stayed with them, but being of service to their family was another way I changed poison into medicine. I loved doing housework, and whether they realized it or not, my friends needed the help.

I'm a great cleaner and organizer, and in those days, when I stayed with friends while I was getting back on my feet, I enjoyed making their homes shine. I felt useful, and my life condition rose as a result.

The best way to attain Buddhahood
is to encounter a good friend.
How far can our own wisdom take us?
If we have even enough wisdom
to distinguish hot from cold,
we should seek out a good friend.

—NICHIREN

•

Having good friends and advancing together
with them is not half the Buddha way
but all the Buddha way.

—SHAKYAMUNI

•

To not advance is to retreat.

—TSUNESABURO MAKIGUCHI

Back in the kitchen, Wayne asked me again, "If you could have anything your heart truly desires, what would you want? For yourself, for the people you love, for your community, for the world."

I didn't know how to answer that question. I was on my own for the first time and the future I wanted wasn't entirely in focus yet.

Whatever your circumstances, it's a valuable exercise to ask yourself these questions. What would your version of ideal happiness look like? What is your heart's desire?

When I was in my twenties and early thirties, I didn't know what I wanted and hadn't really thought about where I was going. I just went.

It may seem obvious, but if you don't know what you want, how can you possibly get it? If you don't know what your idea of fulfillment is, then it will be difficult to find. It's like setting out on a trip without a destination. If you don't have a clear destination, then you'll likely end up wandering. Sometimes wandering can be fun for a short time, but eventually it becomes frustrating and aimless. And an aimless path isn't a suitable foundation for a joyful life.

Since I didn't have an answer for Wayne at that time, he suggested I create a mission statement for my life, to help set a clear direction. With a mission statement, I could see how the things I began to dream about would support my mission in life.

I dug deeper and deeper within, letting go of what was holding me back, and began to see myself more clearly.

That's when I saw what had to change for me to be happy and successful. When I could see myself clearly, I knew I could change anything.

This is the essence of chanting Nam-myoho-renge-kyo. Once I understood this, I intensified my practice. That's when I started chanting several hours per day.

I was finally on the path to revealing my true self. By raising my life condition, I gained clarity and strength to find the best way forward and change every poison I faced into medicine.

If you haven't created a mission statement for your life, I encourage you to do so, and be candid with yourself about what you value and what you truly want. It's all right if the gap between reality and your dreams is big. I think that's how it should be. As Einstein said, we should pursue goals that we can "just barely achieve through our greatest efforts."

When life is difficult, returning to your mission statement will remind you of your purpose, your vow, and help raise your life condition.

When our life condition is high enough, anything is possible—including the impossible. The key is to keep moving forward, even if only in the tiniest steps, with the solid belief that you will absolutely get where you want to go.

Remove all doubt from your mind.

And remember that the "how" isn't as important as the "what."

After I embraced Buddhism, I never doubted I would get to where I wanted to go. But much of the time I had no idea how exactly I would get there. I left the "how" up to the universe and the mystical workings of my mind and soul.

All along, I kept this encouragement from Daisaku Ikeda close to my heart: "One thing is certain: The power of belief, the power of thought, will move reality in the direction of what we believe and conceive of it. If you really believe you can do something, you can. That is a fact. When you clearly envision the outcome of victory, engrave it upon your heart, and are firmly convinced that you will attain it, your brain makes every effort to realize the mental image you have created. And then, through your unceasing efforts, that victory is finally made a reality."

As I worked on mastering my mind in this way, and approached obstacles as catalysts for growth, continually changing poison into medicine without complaint, I experienced a deep-seated shift.

Miracles didn't happen overnight. But with patience and persistence, miraculous transformations built up within me. Gradually, improvements in my external environment came about, too, reflecting those inner transformations.

The cold darkness of winter that had blanketed so many years of my inner world finally started giving way to a warm, bright spring.

That's when my real evolution, my revolution, began.

Chapter Six

A Revolution
of the Heart

Sunlight streamed through the window as I sipped my morning tea. Crystal figurines on the table caught the light, scattering a cascade of colors across my wall. These rays of golden light had departed from the sun about eight minutes earlier and traveled some 93 million miles to reach the room where I sat.

In another moment or two, this precious spectacle would end. But I was, and am, thankful that the grand light show of our planet's beloved star will go on for billions of years to come. It's just another ordinary miracle we're fortunate to witness on this paradise we call Earth.

For many years—nearly two decades, in fact—I was blind to the beauty of such simple wonders of nature. It was there, all around me, of course; I hadn't left the planet. But, in a way, I felt as if I had left this world, as unhealthy influences had enveloped me like a dense fog. The beauty of the world had become unrecognizable to me.

Symptoms of my negative karma dragged my life condition down so low that, for me, basic existence was a chore. I had lost the joy of being alive.

Life, in all its glorious, yet subtle, manifestations, is a priceless gift. Simple, unadorned life holds an abundant inheritance of hope from Mother Earth, the birthright of us all. I'm often reminded of Nichiren's words: "Life itself is the most precious of all treasures. Even one extra day of life is worth more than ten million coins of gold."

Yet, we can easily forget to appreciate the beauty of our lives when we are caught up in hectic routines of work, school, or relationships. It can become even harder when we're faced with responsibilities, deadlines, bills, and people struggling to solve their own problems.

At one time or another, many of us withdraw into our shell, hoping to protect ourselves from the discomforts of daily life, not to mention the greater challenges from the four universal sufferings of birth, sickness, aging, and death. Even if we don't hide in our shell, there's another familiar place we may retreat to: our comfort zone.

In both cases, we aren't challenging ourselves to grow.

We have a saying in the Buddhist community: If you aren't moving forward, then you're actually going backward because everything in the universe is always in flux. That means if you aren't striving to advance in some area of your life, watch out: You may be moving backward without even realizing it.

That was the case with me before I started chanting. I mistook material fortune—my fame, a nice home, designer clothes, expensive cars—for moving forward in life. What I eventually learned is that, despite these outward trappings of success, I was actually moving backward in the only area that really matters—my inner life condition. This manifested in a number of ways. I lost interest in improving myself. Performing, which I once loved, became a burden. I didn't like how I looked, didn't like my voice, didn't like doing interviews, didn't like much of anything. The truth was, I didn't like me.

That is, until I discovered the powerfully freeing wisdom of "human revolution." For the past forty-seven years, I've used this process of inner transformation to unlock the joyous potential of my life.

Too many revolutions throughout history have cost the lives of many people and brought misery to society. Human revolution is quite different.

By revitalizing myself each day, my life condition improved, and I moved forward within myself, even if just a step at a time. I achieved new heights of creativity and gained a new awareness of the sanctity of my own life and the lives of all around me. This is the best kind of revolution I can imagine.

Human revolution is stable and internal. It is a revolution of the heart.

It's the process of personal growth through challenge—what happens when we challenge ourselves to expand our capabilities.

This most humane type of all revolutions helped me to break apart the hard outer shell of my egotistic "lesser self" and reveal the "greater self" that exists within all of us. That greater self is the indestructible, eternal part of each of us that is capable of limitless wisdom, courage, and compassion.

In my family's Baptist heritage, such a revolution of the heart is described as being "born again." I've heard prominent Christian preachers tell the story of Jesus and his forty days and forty nights in the wilderness, which they say catalyzed his human revolution. Because when Jesus returned, he was transformed.

Fortunately, we do not have to disappear in the desert for forty days and nights to experience change. I've found that human revolution doesn't have to be something extraordinary or divorced from daily life. For example:

Let's say there's a high school girl who has never been an A student, but decides to challenge herself by taking subjects she finds difficult, like French.

That girl was me.

I knew I wouldn't be great at a foreign language, and I didn't need to take those classes, but I wanted to challenge my limitations.

Or, let's say there's a young woman who prefers to be a loner. Socializing in groups isn't comfortable for her, but she challenges herself by joining sports teams, social clubs, and volunteering to plan student events.

That young lady was me, too.

I loved being alone more than anything when I was young. I could happily entertain myself all day long. But as high school approached, I sensed that standing on the sidelines wouldn't help me much, so I made an effort to move out of my comfort zone.

I joined the track team and the basketball team, and became a cheerleader. I played basketball with my team, then rushed to change into my cheerleading outfit and come back out to lead the cheers! I also volunteered to organize school dances and other student activities.

These are some of my earliest experiences with human revolution and getting comfortable with voluntary growth.

Stepping out of your comfort zone is a lifelong practice, and I'm happy to say that it's also a surefire way to add fulfilling new dimensions to your life; wonderful things happen when you open your heart and mind to new possibilities.

For example, people who saw my stage persona often assumed that I was comfortable with being a so-called sex symbol. That wasn't the case at all.

Being thought of in that way was completely out of my comfort zone. I had to consciously work at being comfortable with that image.

The most sacred place
isn't the church, the mosque, or the temple,
it's the temple of the body.
That's where spirit lives.

–SUSAN TAYLOR

•

The kingdom of God is within you.

–LUKE 17:21

•

More valuable than treasures in a storehouse
are treasures of the body, and the treasures of the heart
are the most valuable of all.

–NICHIREN

I didn't want to reject the "sex symbol" view of me, since people seemed to like it, so I decided to make that persona mine. I owned it by playing mostly to my female fans, not to the men in the audience, and I did this for two reasons. I didn't want the women at my shows to feel uncomfortable because they thought I was going after their men. And I wanted to encourage women to reveal their own "phenomenal woman," as Maya Angelou wrote in her poem by that name.

The truth is, you can challenge yourself to find a higher purpose in anything you do at work, or in life. Then you can own it, embrace it, and do your best at it. That is human revolution.

Believe it or not, choosing songs for my albums has also been an exercise in growth. There have been songs I initially disliked and didn't want to sing that ultimately became big hits for me. I had to open my mind, partly because I trusted my manager Roger's keen ear for a hit, but also because I decided to step outside my comfort zone and give something unfamiliar a chance.

When I did that, I began to hear deeper meaning and greater potential in songs that I had rejected hastily. In the process of opening up to something that was initially uncomfortable, I made the songs my own, adding nuances that communicated a different meaning and subtext to my audiences and expanded the song's potential, along with my own.

Before committing to a song, I have to visualize how I

might perform it onstage. I imagine it from start to finish before recording a single word. If the song ends up being a hit, I'll have to sing it over and over, and I want to make sure it will have meaning for me and my audiences for years to come.

Going through this process and stretching my boundaries is how I created some of my most successful songs and performances. And I'm grateful that I did.

Could you imagine my career without "What's Love Got to Do with It"? That was my biggest hit, and by far the most beloved and transformational song for me and for my fans.

But it was one of the songs I didn't like when I first heard it! If I hadn't been willing to go outside my comfort zone, open my mind a little wider, and do the extra work it took to make it mine, who knows if I would have broken through in my career.

A more recent example: When I was approached with the idea of a musical theater production about my life, I wasn't interested. There were many reasons for me to say no. I had just retired, and the last thing I wanted was more work. I was a little uncomfortable with the idea of stage actors performing my story. Frankly, I couldn't imagine why people would want to see it. But I decided to venture outside my comfort zone once again and go for it.

I'm glad I did. Developing *Tina: The Tina Turner Musical* turned out to be rewarding and cathartic. It has given me a deeper appreciation of my accomplishments and complete peace with my past, and audiences on both sides of the Atlantic have responded positively.

Even this book that you're holding in your hands is an exercise in human revolution.

Putting together a spiritual exploration like this has been a dream of mine for decades, but I wasn't sure if I could write this kind of material well, so I held back. Honestly, the voice of a girl who sometimes struggled in school (me) popped into my head and questioned whether I was capable of doing it. I'm grateful for the encouragement of my trusted coauthors, who supported me to break through my self-doubt and have helped me to organize and express my thoughts.

Falling in love with my husband, Erwin, was another exercise in leaving my comfort zone, of being open to the unexpected gifts that life has to offer. The day I first met Erwin, at an airport in Germany, I should have been too tired from my flight, too preoccupied with thoughts of my concert tour, and in too much of a hurry to get to my hotel to pay much attention to the young music executive who came from my record company to welcome me. But I did notice him, and I instantly felt an emotional connection.

Even then, I could have ignored what I felt—I could have listened to the ghost voices in my head telling me that I didn't look good that day, or that I shouldn't be thinking about romance because it never ends well. Instead, I listened to my heart. I left my comfort zone and made it a priority to get to know Erwin. That simple first meeting led to a long, beautiful relationship—and my one true marriage.

As you can see from my life, human revolution is really just the conscious elevation of your outlook beyond your everyday world and striving to achieve something more expansive and meaningful. It's what happens when you grow beyond your comfort zone.

Ask yourself this simple question:

Will I take a step forward, or will I stay where I am now?

Your answer to that question, moment by moment, determines your life path.

It might seem counterintuitive, but as we discussed in the last chapter, it is precisely when you experience the worst problems and face seemingly impossible odds that you gain the most valuable opportunities to bring about your human revolution, to break through your limitations, and to change poison into medicine.

When I was going through some of my hardest times, perhaps it would have felt easier to give in to quick fixes, like smoking, alcohol, or drugs. Instead I chose to look inward, to tap the wellspring of my greater self.

Rather than self-medicate, I chose to self-motivate. I took action. I went to my spiritual side for help, studying and practicing Buddhism, which made me strong. And I sought to make my body healthier by researching the best nourishment, a plant-based diet, and holistic remedies. I chose self-improvement, even if it seemed like the harder path. That's human revolution.

I'm not trying to sound like a superhero. There were times when my resolve was challenged, and I had to reset.

As I write this now in my eighties, I can say to you with absolute assurance that a lifetime can zip by in what feels like only a few turns of a kaleidoscope. Unless we make conscious efforts to achieve our own personal human revolution, too many of us end up spending our precious days just busily running around, but never getting anywhere.

We remain stuck in the lower worlds—consumed by ego, fears, and desires in the shallow realm of our lesser self.

But when we do our best to lift ourselves up by increasing our self-love, thoughtfulness, and kindness in all our behaviors, we can then live out a true revolution of the heart.

I believe that, for much of human history, there has been a common, yet deluded, belief that the key to happiness is found in controlling or changing our external world, our environment, our economies, our politics, or our social structures. We humans have devoted a lot of time and energy to these endeavors, while dedicating far less effort to transforming our internal world, which is what dictates the way we actually live our lives.

We end up chasing after things outside ourselves that have little value, while disregarding the source of real value—our own hearts. I pray for the day when our collective efforts will correct this imbalance, bring about a "valuing of the valuable," and raise the curtain on a global human revolution.

Love stretches your heart and
makes you big inside.
—MARGARET WALKER

•

I have an everyday religion that works for me.
Love yourself first, and everything else falls into line.
—LUCILLE BALL

•

Tell me who you love
and I'll tell you who you are.
—CREOLE PROVERB

When I see the word *revolution,* I think of dramatic change. In our daily lives, however, a gradual change over the span of years as we mature is a more typical progression.

And yet, I've discovered through my own experience that human revolution arises when we accelerate our typical pace of growth and undergo a relatively rapid change for the better. Like a supersonic flight on a spiritual plane within.

As I began to experience my own revolution, I found it important to remember that my daily choices and changes in my actions matter the most. Lasting changes, in our own lives and in society, are only possible through changes of the heart. There must be a transformation in our thoughts, words, and deeds, a change of intention, to become better today than we were yesterday.

For me, and millions of people around the world, the catalyst for this process is the daily practice of chanting Nam-myoho-renge-kyo, which affirms the sacredness of all life and the conviction that we all have God within us.

This is the first book I've written about my spiritual practice and the important internal lessons I've learned. But for decades now, I've done my best to encourage others and to teach through my actions, so that my experiences may be of help to them.

Since I began my solo career—thousands of concerts in dozens of countries—I have chanted and prayed before each show, focusing on the happiness of each person who came to see me. I visualized my audience and prayed that I could be whoever each person needed me to be that day in order to inspire their dreams, invigorate their hope, and recharge their souls. I prayed to spark in them a joyful revolution of the heart.

I believe prayer is a positive, powerful action that anyone can take at any time. It is much more constructive than lamenting our circumstances, or the circumstances of others. I've learned that when battling challenges, complaining doesn't help.

In chapter five, I spoke of the wonderful older Japanese ladies who were in my neighborhood chanting group when I first started my Buddhist practice. They'd bring us the most delicious rice balls and green tea. One day, as we sat around after our chanting session, enjoying these delicacies and talking about our challenges, I recall them saying: "Complaints erase good fortune. Never complain!"

I totally agree. I've never complained about my circumstances. What good comes from complaints? Grumbling only brings you down. Find a way forward, smile, shake it off, love yourself. Use your challenges to become stronger. This is how you can transform your karma and open your heart.

There's a saying that there are two things you should never worry about: the things you can change, and the things you can't. In my experience, virtually anything can be transformed by changing yourself first, so don't worry. As long as your behavior is grounded in compassion, and you're continually polishing your own life, you're on the best path.

Sometimes, our innate Buddha nature, which encompasses our compassion, clarity, and open-mindedness, can become tarnished from lack of use. But when we step out of our comfort zone and open our hearts, we can polish away the tarnish and radiate clear light into our world.

By extension, this path of polishing our own heart increases our confidence in our human family's ability to overcome conflicts and global challenges, individually and collectively, to change our world for the better.

As you build up your own history of achieving inner changes to change your external circumstances, you will also develop faith in your ability to transform even seemingly impossible difficulties into benefits for yourself and others.

As I write this, my personal history of conscious human revolution is clocking in at nearly half a century. Though I believe there is no pain-free path to self-improvement, the rewards—independence, self-reliance, and freedom—are worth the effort. I'm confident you will gain the same.

It's never too late to start, or to accelerate, your own human revolution.

I really do believe that age is just a number, and I have never let age stand in my way. Not at forty-two, when people said that I was too old to be a rock star. And not now, in my eighties, when the book I dreamed of writing for decades is finally in your hands.

I've passed eighty, but I have not "arrived," because I still challenge myself to grow, to step out of my comfort zone, to improve my life, and to be of service to others.

It's all right if you don't have a role model in your life to inspire you. I didn't grow up with role models of civility and charm, so I worked with what I had. I found them in the movie theater, as I sat in the darkened auditorium, studying the qualities of the characters in the films. There were role models in books, too, where heroic figures in novels and history showed me that anything was possible. I also found them in my own imagination, where I visualized creating a life that was higher than my life condition, although I didn't know what Buddhism was at the time or have the words to express those concepts.

I visualized traveling the world, doing great things, and living in a home where I would be surrounded by beauty and love. Even after my parents moved away, and I was bounced around from one relative's home to another, I decorated my makeshift rooms as best I could because I knew instinctively that I needed dignity in my life.

There was no one pushing me to live a better life, or to dream; it was something I wanted for myself, and that desire fueled my seeking spirit. Through the losses and neglect of my childhood, the turmoil of my first marriage, and the battles to extricate myself from that and start over, I never gave up.

There were never any limitations to my imagination. Visualization served me well—in my mind's eye, I always saw a better life. Imagination, visualizing, and dreaming big, combined with hard work, determination, and faith, are what got me where I wanted to go, and they can do the same for you.

If you ever find your resolve melting away, tell yourself, "This time I'll do it! This time I'll win!" As long as you keep moving forward, despite any disappointments and setbacks, you will be on the path to victory.

I've observed people who veered from the path of self-improvement, having been swayed by short-term outlooks, failures, or by the opinions of others. In every case, their life condition suffered. Thankfully, I've known many more people who strived to improve themselves and work for the greater good. Invariably, their lives became more fulfilling.

It boils down to a matter of choices—making thoughtful decisions toward improvement, for yourself and for others—and the intention behind those choices. At every moment, we always have a choice, even if it feels as if we don't. Sometimes that choice may simply be to think a more positive thought.

Remember that cultivating the deepest dimension of yourself, your inward journey, is always the most direct path to happiness.

So, let's rev up our humanity, and rev up our lives. Think of the *rev* in the word *revolution* as meaning you have the opportunity to accelerate the speed of your human revolution and rev it up. I know you'll be happy you did.

We need a revolution inside our own minds.
—JOHN HENRIK CLARKE

•

Through our scientific and technological genius,
we have made of this world a neighborhood and yet
we have not had the ethical commitment
to make of it a brotherhood.
But somehow . . . we must all learn
to live together as brothers
or we will all perish together as fools.
—MARTIN LUTHER KING JR.

•

Revolution really must occur within.
—ALICE WALKER

My Buddhist faith has been the foundation of my personal path toward revolution. But you don't have to be a Buddhist to benefit from these principles.

In fact, you don't have to be a Buddhist to be a Buddha. As Daisaku Ikeda says, "When we realize that our lives are one with the great and eternal life of the universe, we are the Buddha. The purpose of Buddhism is to enable all people to come to this realization."

This mind-set is open to everyone, regardless of religion or cultural background.

The Lotus Sutra's ancient wisdom belongs to all humanity, proclaiming that each person equally possesses the Buddha nature, with infinite potential and inherent dignity, lighting the way to true independence and absolute happiness for everyone.

To me, it is a simple understanding that our salvation is up to us, and that we must practice what we preach. To express it another way, it is the realization that we ordinary beings are capable of miraculous transformations when we strive to polish ourselves. Whenever I think about this, I feel empowered. "God helps those who help themselves," as the saying goes.

It's not because I am special that I was able to make miracles happen in my life. I am no different from any other person. My story is just better known because I live under a spotlight. People you've never heard of are making miracles happen in their own lives every day.

I call something a miracle when an ordinary person achieves something extraordinary. We all have the potential to create miraculous changes. It is my hope and my prayer that you will become a miracle maker, a "human revolutionist," too.

My favorite Baptist voice of our time, Rev. Dr. Lawrence Carter Sr., founding dean of the Martin Luther King Jr. International Chapel at Morehouse College, said: "I have no doubt that in the twenty-first century the term *human revolution* will take root in the Western spiritual vernacular. Human revolution means an inner reformation from ignorance of one's own divinity to a profound awareness of the Buddha or Christ nature within—from selfishness to selflessness, from limited prospects to limitless possibilities."

As I learned when I first began my study of Buddhism decades ago, the roots of this concept date back thousands of years to the Lotus Sutra, regarded the world over as the Buddha's ultimate teaching, and to the earliest Buddhist philosophers who were his disciples.

But it wasn't until the twentieth century, during World War II, that an educator in Japan named Josei Toda began teaching about "human revolution." I first heard about this great man from Herbie Hancock at one of my neighborhood chanting meetings in the late 1970s.

Herbie explained how Josei Toda, a student of the Lotus Sutra, became convinced that its wisdom would guide people to achieve a revolution of the heart, which in turn would lead to a rejection of violence of any sort. Toda devoted his life to the cause of peace and was imprisoned for two years by the militarist Japanese government for his unshakable antiwar stance.

I was deeply touched by a vision of the ancient Lotus Sutra's message of enlightened transformation traveling across land, sea, and time to a peaceful teacher in a wartime jail cell. Toda was just one determined person whose intention to share this empowering truth with humanity was so pure it would eventually spread across the globe, reaching people like me, and now you.

I hope that this message will be as powerful a tool for you as it has been for me.

My dear friend David Bowie, who had a lifelong interest in Buddhism, used to call me a phoenix, the mythical bird who rises from the ashes. I believe what he saw in me was none other than the regenerative power of human revolution. The Lotus Sutra's wisdom enabled changes within me that called to mind a phoenix, burning away the old and rising up in the new, casting off the transient and revealing the true.

Rising from the ashes of my earlier life, I learned that our thoughts, words, and deeds are unified through spiritual practice. They are made whole within us. And when our thoughts, words, and deeds are aligned with our most positive intentions, magic happens.

We go from a limping, fragmented self to a soaring, unified self. We become healed and whole, within and without.

I learned how to heal myself through my spiritual practice of polishing my life. By studying the wisdom of the Lotus Sutra, I became my soul's doctor.

I discovered how to break through the confines of the lower worlds and my lesser self, the private and isolated self that was a prisoner of fears, desires, and illusions. I broke these chains by practicing self-mastery, self-reformation, and refining my character. I learned to bow in deep respect to my own Buddha nature, and I found that when I bowed to the Buddha nature in others, just like facing a mirror, they bowed in return.

Embracing the Quaker philosophy that no one individual should be prized over another, I try to treat everyone with respect, regardless of their status or background. I hope you do, too.

Through these universal practices, I'm convinced that anyone can transform the three poisons of humankind—greed, anger, and foolishness—into altruism, compassion, and enlightenment. We can all move from the lower conditions of our inner life state to higher, happier ones.

Best of all, you don't have to seek this wisdom on some distant mountaintop. Rather, you can find it within yourself, beneath your own feet, so to speak. A well-known, ancient Buddhist passage says: "You are your own master. Could anyone else be your master? When you have gained control over yourself, you have found a master of rare value."

This passage urges us to live independently, true to ourselves and unswayed by others. This greater, cosmic self is the Buddha nature, or Christ consciousness, within every one of us. It is what I believe Ralph Waldo Emerson envisioned when he wrote of the "universal beauty, to which every part and particle is equally related; the eternal One."

To me, a revolution of the heart means a change of being, attitude, potential, and a sense of social and global responsibility. When we experience a true revolution of the heart, we understand that differences of race, nationality, or culture do not need to create divisions or confrontations. The limitations in our own hearts and minds tear us apart, from ourselves and from others.

I have witnessed people categorize others, or even themselves, through the narrow lens of gender, age, nationality or ethnicity, habits, personality, and more. It can be tough to separate who we really are from these limited characteristics, which are often tangled together. Looking beyond these surface descriptions helps us to reveal our true identity and is another important part of our human revolution.

As I shared earlier, I've faced the obstacles of ageism, racism, sexism, and other forms of prejudice; even nationalism. During my career comeback in the late 1970s and early 1980s, when I performed all over the world, people asked why I, an American, wanted to work in countries other than my homeland.

My response (with a wink) was, "What's nationality got to do with it?"

What I am is a humanist before anything...
and my beliefs are for the human race,
they don't exclude anyone.
—WHOOPI GOLDBERG

•

Religion without humanity
is very poor human stuff.
—SOJOURNER TRUTH

Thanks to my own hard-won revolution of the heart, I now have positive, proud feelings about overcoming discrimination; but the scourge of divisiveness is still a prevalent, serious matter. As Martin Luther King Jr. said, to resolve such deep-rooted biases "we must undergo a radical revolution of values."

The ancient sages who first explained the "greater self" that emerges through human revolution also shed light on the poison of prejudice, and how to reform fundamental societal values. They did so by illuminating the concepts of "dependent origination" and "the oneness of life and its environment."

Those terms may sound complicated, but they really aren't. Simply put, dependent origination means that, whether in human society or in nature, nothing exists in isolation. "No man is an island," the poet John Donne famously said. We are all connected in some way to everyone and everything, as we are all made up of the same sacred mystery of universal energy.

We are all made of stardust. We are all children of God, related in Buddha consciousness, one extended family of living beings sharing a singular home, Earth.

I love when Beyoncé reminded the class of 2020 during her virtual commencement address to "lead with heart." I believe we must make kindness a practice, a vow, a commitment.

I do my best to treat everyone with kindness and respect, especially the hardworking people in the healthcare, retail, hospitality, maintenance, and service industries. I know from fans who work in these jobs that they are often treated unkindly. Maybe this is because they are less inclined or able to speak up for themselves, or because people who benefit from their labor think they can get away with being disrespectful.

When my friends Wayne and Ana Maria Shorter welcomed me and my boys when we had no place to go, I showed my gratitude and love by cooking healthful meals for them and cleaning their home. I enjoyed doing that for them and took pride in being of service.

I have deep gratitude and respect for my own staff, the wonderful people who take care of me and my home. I compensate them well and I take every opportunity I can to show them respect and appreciation, even if it's just serving them water, or tea, or a sandwich. Although they could get these things for themselves, I sometimes like to do it for them as an expression of loving kindness.

I have always seen great value in practicing kindness. Although I had no money to buy gifts as a child, I gave my friends the gift of song to cheer them up.

Depending on the situation, I'd sing to them and make up melodies and lyrics on the spot about whatever was going on in their lives. If a girlfriend was lonely or heartbroken, I'd make up a song about the handsome and adoring boyfriend I imagined coming into her life. Or if a friend felt deprived or neglected, I'd make up a song about a gift of a shiny new doll, or a velvet party dress, that I knew would make her happy.

It costs nothing to be kind but could mean the world to those who receive it.

Which takes us back to our human revolution.

If we don't like the society we see around us, the timeless Buddhist concept of the oneness of life and its environment teaches that it's up to us to change ourselves first. This means that we must be the change we wish to see. We may think of ourselves and our surroundings as separate, like islands that appear to be separated by vast stretches of water. Yet, just as islands are connected to one another under the ocean surface, we are all completely intertwined.

Nichiren compared this interconnectedness, or oneness, of our life and surroundings to our body and its shadow. If you don't like the way your shadow looks, how can you most easily change it? By moving yourself.

This may seem simplistic, but it is a tremendously empowering insight. It explains that everything around us, including our relationships and our work, reflects our inner state of life. And it encourages us to understand that we can transform any situation through our own inner change.

In this light, it is clear how foolish and harmful discrimination of any sort is, both for those carrying the prejudice and for those they act against.

My heartfelt wish is that you and I, and everyone around the world, will continue expanding our hearts and minds while celebrating our differences and ridding ourselves of any form of discrimination. This, I believe, is a basic requirement for peace, both within ourselves and in our societies.

Through my Buddhist practice, I've come to see that every living being has fundamental value. In realizing my own value, I recognize the value of all others. And I see that each of us is a microcosm of the world. By transforming ourselves, the microcosm, we contribute to changing the shared karma and destiny of the whole human race and the natural world we occupy, the macrocosm. That is the ultimate expression of human revolution.

There is no greater responsibility and honor than this.

人間
Ningen

革命
Kakumei

In Japanese script, the characters used to write the term "human revolution" are drawn in four distinct symbols (Japanese: *ningen kakumei*). The first two characters, which represent "human," originated thousands of years ago in Buddhist texts depicting the realm of humanity. They show a person by a gate, the space filled with sunlight. The next two characters represent "revolution," with the first conveying the meaning of changing or reforming, paired with the symbol for life or one's state of life, which also represents destiny. This paints a beautiful image of undergoing our human revolution, as we activate our light-filled inner realm to change our life and destiny.

Chapter Seven

BEYOND SINGING

I t was a summer afternoon in 2008. As the rain clouds hovering over Lake Zürich slowly parted to make way for glorious sunshine, a rainbow appeared over my home. This awe-inspiring sight suggested to me that something deeply meaningful would come from this day. I believe in heavenly signs and good omens from Mother Nature. To me, rainbows symbolize peace, diversity, and awakenings.

This glorious rainbow heralded the arrival of my good friend Regula Curti.

Earlier that day, she had called from a retreat in the Swiss mountains. Usually, I don't answer the house phone, but for some reason, I did. It was destiny. If anyone else had answered, they'd have taken a message, and I might not have responded in a timely way because I was going overseas the next morning. As I'd soon discover, time was of the essence.

As we exchanged warm hellos, I heard an emotional undercurrent in Regula's voice and sensed she had something important to say.

"Sounds like something's on your mind," I said.

I could almost hear her smile as she replied, "Yes, there is, something special."

Instead of continuing the conversation on the phone, I suggested that we speak in person that very day.

Regula happily agreed. I prefer face-to-face, heart-to-heart communication because it's more personal.

Regula and I have known each other for two decades, and have shared special times together, from performing a spontaneous song and dance for a friend's birthday on a boat in the Mediterranean to enjoying dinner parties at each other's homes. Over the years, she and I have also bonded over long discussions about spirituality and the healing power of music and singing. I was curious to hear what she wanted to share with me.

Regula must have flown down that mountain—she arrived amazingly fast—and pulled into my driveway. As I stepped outside to welcome her, the heavens cast seven colors above our heads.

Sitting down to enjoy tea in my living room, she explained that she had been developing an idea for an album of Buddhist and Christian prayers to promote peace and understanding among cultures. This would be the first album from Beyond Music, a multicultural project Regula had founded the year before.

Intriguing, I thought as my mind flashed back to a seer who many years earlier had told me I'd someday work with an interfaith group of women. These aspirations were dear to my heart, and I wanted to know more.

She said that production of the album was already underway with the Tibetan Buddhist singer Dechen Shak-Dagsay, who also lives by Lake Zürich. The previous year, I'd attended a wonderful event that Dechen and Regula had facilitated—an interfaith dialogue between the Dalai Lama of Tibet and Abbot Martin Werlen of Switzerland.

"That day of dialogue was so moving," Regula said, "that it inspired this album."

One comment by the Dalai Lama that had resonated with her that day was: "It is important to be open and tolerant toward other beliefs, and to always respect one another despite any differences between religions."

Dechen and Regula carried that sentiment forward and were now weaving together Buddhist and Christian mantras into an inspirational album. As the recordings progressed, they realized the project would benefit from a celebrity to help promote its messages.

"This morning while I was meditating," Regula continued, "I heard your voice, Tina. But you weren't singing—you were speaking, sharing a spiritual message on the album."

That was all I needed to know. "I've been waiting for

this moment for a long time," I told her. "Since the 1980s, I've been saying that I'd someday do a spiritual project. The moment is now. I want to be a part of it."

The timing was perfect. I had just announced the final tour of my career, celebrating my fiftieth year in music. At the age of sixty-nine, I had committed to an ambitious tour schedule with ninety shows around the world, and more than 1.2 million tickets sold. What a way to bring my career to a close!

Preparations for my 50th Anniversary Tour were well underway when I joined Regula's team in the studio. I would have just enough time to complete my recordings for the album before I departed for Missouri to launch the tour. I chose Missouri as the starting point for my farewell tour, since that's where my professional career had begun exactly half a century earlier.

The album, titled *Buddhist and Christian Prayers,* was to be released in June 2009, about a month after my world tour ended.

The fundamental spirit of the Beyond Music movement is unity in diversity, which seamlessly aligns with my spiritual practice. In the Soka Gakkai Buddhist tradition, a beautiful analogy for appreciating diversity is the principle of "cherry, plum, peach, and damson blossoms."

More than 750 years ago, Nichiren taught an all-embracing perspective on diversity by using these fruits to illustrate that everyone, without regard to race, gender, orientation, and so on, possesses the Buddha nature equally. His words remind us that the Lotus Sutra embraces all living beings, without distinction, highlighting that every single one of us has great worth and inherent potential.

In art, pointillism is a good example of this. If you aren't familiar with pointillism, it's a style of painting in which tiny, distinct dots of different colors are applied in patterns to form an image. A famous example is Georges Seurat's painting *A Sunday Afternoon on the Island of La Grande Jatte,* which is on exhibit at the Art Institute of Chicago.

You may recall this artwork from an iconic scene in the film *Ferris Bueller's Day Off,* when the character of Cameron stands transfixed, staring at the painting as the camera zooms in closer and closer, like a microscope, revealing every little dot of color. I remember the first time I visited the Art Institute of Chicago (on "Tina Turner's Day Off") and stood there mesmerized by this painting.

This artistic style honors each color, each dot, for its distinct characteristics. Seurat believed that unifying diverse colors in this way made his art more brilliant and affecting.

I see humanity the same way.

By honoring each other's ethnic, religious, and cultural backgrounds, we become stronger and happier, brightening the cosmic masterpiece of artwork that is our world.

Rather than emphasize differences, we should be looking for similarities. Our differences are ultimately superficial, and the best thing to do is celebrate them.

The religious faith that we are born into is largely determined by the region where we live and the ethnic background of our family. In my case, I was born to an African American family in the southern region of the United States. Like most families of our description, we embraced the Baptist religious tradition.

Although I went from Baptist to Buddhist, I've honored my family's heritage and cherish the similarities between these two paths.

Baptist teachings encouraged me to work toward attaining admission into a heavenly paradise, while Buddhism inspires me to attain the enduring and enlightened life condition of Buddhahood. Although the goals of these two spiritual paths may sound somewhat different, both focus on creating a state of indestructible, eternal happiness. To me, that is an important similarity.

I've met people from all over the world, from many cultures and faiths, and I believe that all religious traditions share the same basic aspirations at their core—to experience everlasting joy by aligning with the positive forces of the universe. We may describe this ultimate reality as Jehovah, God, Allah, Jesus, Hashem, Tao, Brahma, the Creator, the Mystic Law, the Universe, the Force, Buddha nature, Christ consciousness, or any number of other expressions.

When I joined the Beyond project, I made an effort to familiarize myself with diverse faith traditions, as well as learn about the history of exchanges between those spiritual traditions. For example, before recording the album *Buddhist and Christian Prayers,* I had not been aware of any particular contact between the Buddhists and Christians of olden times.

So, I was pleasantly surprised to discover a rich history of interfaith dialogue.

I learned that when Jesuit missionaries first arrived in Japan in the sixteenth century and observed Buddhist ways of thinking and living, they sent back word to Europe that it appeared the Japanese Buddhists had developed an Asian form of Christianity. At the same time, Japanese Buddhists recorded that upon listening to the first European missionaries, they didn't find much about Christian belief to be objectionable; they saw common ground.

For decades, Christian missionaries in Japan lived harmoniously among the largely Buddhist population, until tensions erupted that were rooted in political concerns of the ruling shogunate. It was politics, not religion, that caused discord among the people. This lesson transcends time and is something I wish more of us in today's world would know and understand.

Some two thousand years before the Jesuits landed in Japan, the great Buddhist King Ashoka of India sent out emissaries to distant lands to teach Buddhist ideals of compassion and peace. In the third century B.C.E. (before the Common Era, which is a universal way of delineating time), these envoys recorded in travel logs that among the places they visited were cities in Greece and Egypt, including Alexandria.

Maybe the purpose of being here,
wherever we are, is to increase
the durability and the occasions of love
among and between peoples.

—JUNE JORDAN

•

People can only live fully by helping others to live...
Cultures can only realize their further
richness by honoring other traditions.
And only by respecting natural life can
humanity continue to exist.

—DAISAKU IKEDA

One hundred years before the Buddhist expeditions from India, Alexander the Great opened up avenues of cultural exchange with Indian regions as well. Knowing this, it's easy for me to imagine that Buddhist philosophy must have traveled westward, including to the region where Jesus lived.

Later, Thomas the Apostle explored India and sent tales of Bodhisattvas and Shakyamuni's life to the West. Some of these details made their way into early Christian teachings and evolved into what is now known as the scripture of Saints Barlaam and Josaphat, whose names come from the Sanskrit words for "illustrious Bodhisattva."

Some religious researchers have also traced shared roots between the central message of Christian love and the Buddhist message of compassion.

When my kidneys failed several years ago and I was having dialysis treatments, one of my favorite books to read during treatment was Dante's *The Divine Comedy*. To me, the nine circles of hell Dante describes in the *Inferno* sound like the ancient Buddhist depictions of hellish life conditions and the cause-and-effect relationship between life and life after death.

Recently, I discovered I'm not alone in that view, as modern scholars believe Dante took inspiration from old Buddhist descriptions of infernos and icy places of torment, and then incorporated them into his work.

The desire to seek the essence of the universe has always overflowed the banks of any one cultural or spiritual stream.

With the Beyond project, our vision was to include as many international faith traditions as possible. We began with Buddhism and Christianity—the two faiths closest to our personal experiences. Subsequent albums have continued to expand that vision by including the Hindu traditions of India, as well as traditions from Jewish and Arab cultures.

I wanted to make my spiritual message for the album as universal and inclusive as possible. I just wasn't sure how to go about crafting it. I had dabbled in writing songs about Buddhist concepts in the late 1970s, but I hadn't finished them.

Later, when I met with Buddhist philosopher Daisaku Ikeda, he spoke encouragingly to me about the potential of music to cross cultural boundaries and to inspire a "never give up" spirit in people's lives. I've always believed that music is more than notes on a page; it's a language, something I tried to convey to my band when I said to them, "When you express music from your heart, when you merge it with your soul, the people who hear your artistry will be moved by it so much more."

How could we bring that intention to Beyond?

Since I was on my way to the United States for my tour, I decided to make a quick stop in Carlsbad, California, to ask author Deepak Chopra for advice. I'd read many of his books and have long admired his ability to explain multicultural spiritual concepts to a wide audience.

As I hoped, he was gracious and supportive, and when our visit ended, he gave me a collection of spiritual books to read, assuring me that the right words would come to me at the right time.

I love books, and I spread this new collection around me, feeling like a kid at Christmas. As I started reading, I searched for words and phrases that resonated with me and wrote them on large sheets of paper.

Then, I took all the papers and spread them across my floor. Sitting among these inspirational words, I was basking in a literary garden of positivity. At first, I remained perfectly still and let the wise words around me enter my consciousness through osmosis.

Next, I got up and strolled through my garden of words. I felt chills (or, an "Aha!" moment, as my friend Oprah says) when I hit upon a phrase or word that inspired me.

Maya Angelou, a hero to many of us, believed that "words are things." Words, she felt, hold energy and power. I agree. Words are one of the three types of action (thoughts, words, and deeds) that create karma and affect the condition of our lives.

With this in mind, I chose my words carefully. At the same time, I made the process fun. I started by arranging the sheets I'd gathered into groupings. Sorting them to select my favorites and putting them into just the right order was a playful process. Regula joined me, and we had such a good time that by the end we were giggling like schoolgirls. She suggested that I pin my final selections to the wall and think about them during my daily walks.

Someday we'll be able to measure the power of words.
I think they are things. They get on the walls.
They get in your wallpaper. They get in your rugs,
in your upholstery, and your clothes, and finally into you.
—MAYA ANGELOU

•

Beyond right and wrong there is a field.
I'll meet you there.
—RUMI

Soon, I realized that I wanted to condense the message even further, to the simplest nonsectarian terms. It was important to me that as many people as possible be able to understand the meaning. I wanted to reach anyone who might be struggling in life, anyone who needed inspiration to develop peace and happiness within themselves.

Eventually, I found the precise words I wished to express. As I recorded them, I was amazed to see that the sound engineers and others in the studio were moved to tears by what I said.

In addition to my spoken word message, I've contributed other spiritual recordings to the Beyond project that occupy special places in my heart. For the *Buddhist and Christian Prayers* album, I recorded the beginning of *gongyo,* a selection from the Lotus Sutra that is part of my daily Buddhist prayer routine. For the *Love Within* album, released in 2014, I sang "Amazing Grace," a hymn that I enjoyed singing in church choir as a child. It's still one of my favorites.

Hopefully, the messages I've shared in the Beyond Music albums, like the messages I'm sharing in this book, will continue to touch hearts around the world.

Let me share with you the words I spoke in *Buddhist and Christian Prayers*:

Nothing lasts forever.
No one lives forever.
The flower fades and dies.

Winter passes and spring comes.
Embrace the cycle of life; that is the greatest love.

Go beyond fear. Go beyond fear. Beyond fear takes
you into the place where love grows, where you refuse
to follow the impulses of fear, anger, and revenge.

Beyond means to feel yourself.
Start every day singing like the birds. Singing
takes you beyond, beyond, beyond, beyond . . .

We need a repeated discipline, a genuine training,
to let go of our old habits of mind and to find and
sustain a new way of seeing.

Go beyond the rights and the wrongs.
Prayer clears the head and brings back peace
to the soul. Go beyond to feel the oneness of unity.

Sing! Singing takes you beyond, beyond, beyond,
beyond . . .

We are all the same, all the same. Looking to find
our way back to the source. To the one, to the only one.

Go beyond revenge. The greatest moment in our lives
is when we allow ourselves to teach one another.

Go beyond to feel the oneness of unity. Singing.
Singing takes you beyond, beyond, beyond,
beyond . . .

Take the journey.
Take the journey inside of you.
To become quiet to hear the beyond.
To become patient to receive the beyond.
To become open to invite the beyond in.

Be grateful. Be grateful to allow the beyond.
Be in the present moment, to live in the beyond.

Start every day singing like the birds. Singing
takes you beyond, beyond, beyond, beyond . . .

What does love have to do with it?
Love grows when you trust.
When you trust, love heals and renews.

Love inspires and empowers us to do great things.
And makes us a better person to love. Love makes us
feel safe and brings us closer to God.

When you go beyond, that's where you find true love.
Keep singing. Singing takes you beyond, beyond,
beyond, beyond . . .

Without a song, each day would be a century.

—MAHALIA JACKSON

•

Music can give you the strength to change,
or to fight for a cause, for your family, for yourself.
Music can give you the strength to stand up and face
your trials. When you sometimes feel utterly discouraged,
you can, thanks to music, summon the strength to rise up
and once again strive to carry on with all your might.

—WAYNE SHORTER

My beloved home on Lake Zürich is called Château Algonquin. The house was given that name long before my husband, Erwin, and I moved into it in the 1990s, and we weren't sure what *Algonquin* meant. We asked our neighbors, but no one seemed to know. After some investigating, we found out it's a word that the French derived from a Native American expression meaning "they are our relatives" or "they are our allies."

The idea that our home is named for a sentiment of unity was happy news. Unity is an important message to me because I believe that we are all related, and all allies.

The wisdom of the Lotus Sutra has deepened my awareness of the interconnectedness of all life, showing me that it is only the limited capacity of our senses that causes people to place importance on arbitrary separations between "us" and "them."

Buddhism teaches that all living beings have been one another's mother, father, sister, brother, child, or other loved one, many times over, spanning infinite lifetimes throughout every corner of the universe. Whether we can fathom this concept or not, I hope the idea opens your mind, as it has opened mine.

Here we all are, together again, living on this wonderful planet. That's our reality. So, let's act like the extended family we actually are, and always behave kindly. To quote Pope Francis: "Today, more than ever, the world needs a revolution of tenderness."

I've witnessed the transformative power of singing prayers together in multicultural unity, which helps us to connect on a spiritual level—a place of love and respect where worldly differences fade. Music is a universal bridge between "you" and "me," "us" and "them."

I feel strongly that it is time for the world to move beyond division into greater spiritual connection. We must be united to collectively solve the problems we face.

As Martin Luther King Jr. said: "We are all caught in an inescapable network of mutuality, tied in a single garment of destiny. Whatever affects one directly, affects all indirectly . . . This is the interrelated structure of reality."

Whether you practice Buddhism as I do, or you have another form of spiritual practice, or even if you're not spiritually inclined at all, I believe the most important thing for the survival and prosperity of the human race is for all of us to unite in a shared purpose to preserve this beautiful planet of ours. We must increase our awareness of belonging to the human community, sharing our heavenly oasis not only with one another but with all life on Earth.

As physicist Stephen Hawking eloquently explained, it is extremely unlikely that we could ever successfully colonize another hospitable planet, even if we are ever able to identify one. Humans cannot survive the time needed to travel the immense distances required to find other planets like Earth, let alone emigrate to them.

According to Hawking, if we could ever travel at the

speed of light and voyage to the center of our own galaxy and back, Earth would have aged fifty thousand years. That's a trip that doesn't sound very realistic to me.

Rather than fantasizing about the small odds of starting over on another planet, let's focus on reality and direct our energies toward preserving *our* planet, right here, right now.

This can only be achieved by uniting and working together in the shared purpose of solving our mutual problems. To be united with others, we must be united with our own heart—we must be whole within ourselves. Nichiren teaches that individuals at cross-purposes with themselves are certain to end in failure, yet vast numbers of people can attain a shared goal if they are united.

To become whole within, then to unite with others for the greater good, that is the purpose of the words I chose for my spiritual message in *Buddhist and Christian Prayers*.

In my spoken message, in which my voice and soothing music are interwoven, I encourage everyone to sing. Now, I know some of you may be thinking, *Tina, I can't sing! You do the singing, and I'll just listen to you.* But when I say "sing," the voice I am referring to is not necessarily the one you use to sing a song. It's that moment when you find yourself making sounds from within, from your heart.

My Mama Georgie comes to mind for me. Whenever she was in her rocking chair, she would make deep humming sounds—"Hummm." She would sit me on her lap as she hummed, and I loved listening to her. It wasn't a song, just a humming sound. I felt it was the song of her soul.

Sometimes she talked about her grandparents and her great-grandparents, who were part Native American, and stories they told her about the rivers. Perhaps they also taught her to listen to her heartsong and let it out.

"Hummm."

At night, I loved sitting on Mama Georgie's lap, looking up at the stars, listening to her hum. I would hear the hum of the cicadas and the frogs in the distance, and I realized on some level, although I could not have articulated it as a child, that there is a hum, a frequency, a vibration in all of Mother Nature, in the universe. When I grew up and later began my Buddhist practice, the sounds and vibration of Nam-myoho-renge-kyo would remind me of those vibrations of Mama Georgie and nature.

So, when I ask you to sing, I ask that you try to find the unique song, or sound, within you, too. You might find that it's just a "huaaa" or something in falsetto, or your own hum. Any sound that comes from your heart is your very own heartsong.

Singing, I believe, brings out our higher life conditions and helps brighten our environment. Singing helps us to feel beyond happy, opening a flow of joy from within that is impervious to external circumstances.

It makes no difference if you are a good singer with perfect pitch, or if you can't hold a tune. Whatever sounds or songs you enjoy singing, release them and feel your spirit soar!

EXPERIENCE BEYOND MUSIC

Scan these QR codes to visit the
Beyond website and YouTube channel

Chapter Eight

HOMECOMING

In the sanctuary of my Zürich home, I climbed the stairs to my second-floor prayer room to sit at my butsudan, the intricately carved wooden altar where I enjoy chanting every day.

On this particular day, October 13, 2019, there was a beautiful blue autumn sky with puffs of white clouds overhead. Through the glass of my prayer room window, I saw that the trees were turning from their uniform summer green to vibrant golds, reds, and browns.

This special space is where I practice the spiritual work of unknotting the tangled threads of my karma, weaving them into the tapestry of my life's mission.

Lighting the candles to begin my morning prayers, as I have done every day since 1973, I felt my body energizing and my life condition rising from the wellspring of my Buddha nature. The sound of my chanting resonated the chakras within me, getting the wheels turning in my body's energy centers and expressing the vibration of my soul through past, present, and future.

I was tuning in to the divine rhythm of the universe.

As I prayed, I thought of the Broadway musical about my life, which had begun previews the night before. In a few more weeks, Erwin and I were going to New York City for the musical's official opening-night gala. My eightieth birthday would come soon after that.

From the beginning of 2019, I'd enjoyed telling people that I was turning eighty. First, no one could believe it. Or maybe they were just being kind to me! I liked hearing myself say the word *eighty* because part of me wondered if I'd ever make it to that age, and the other part wondered what I'd be like once I got there.

I'm happy to say that, thanks to my dear husband, Erwin, giving me one of his kidneys, the gift of life, I'm in good health and loving life every day.

I'm also thankful that I've not only survived, but *thrived,* so that I can pass on to you this book containing precious gifts that were given to me—the greatest gifts I can offer.

Since so many of my spiritual experiences have centered on "seeing clearly," it's particularly meaningful to me that the first publication of this book is in the year 2020, which I've thought of as "the year of seeing clearly."

After finishing my morning prayers, I joined Erwin for a light brunch of banana, melon, and kiwi slices, together with my favorite German brown bread. We talked about the Broadway opening, which we had been looking forward to for a long time.

During our conversation about the musical, a favorite expression came to mind: "Changing the scenery does not change the script." Using theatrical terms, it means that if you're looking to improve your situation, it's futile to change environments before changing yourself. In other words, you can run from your karma, but if you haven't changed yourself, you can't hide from it.

For years, I'd had a hard time explaining to people why I stayed in my first marriage even after I started practicing Buddhism. I'd like to explain why.

I sensed that until I was ready to get out on my own, until I had built up sufficient internal strength to break free from the negative patterns that had ensnared me, then running away wouldn't make a lasting change. Although it would take some time, I had to save myself from the inside out. Only then would changing the scenery help me.

After Erwin and I finished our brunch, we received word from the musical's producers in New York City that the first preview was a big success. Gratified, I turned my attention to the rest of my day.

To be honest, as soon as I finished my fruit, I was already thinking of what I wanted for supper that night. I hadn't even gotten up from our brunch when I thought, *Maybe I'll make a nice garlic pasta with vegetables and salad.*

I love the simple things in life, like fresh vegetables. That's part of the goodness, the "heart value" I've kept close to me from my earliest days as a country girl. I may look like a grande dame now, but I still think of myself as Anna Mae.

When I was a child, we never wasted anything, especially food. We worked so hard to grow it that we treated it with respect. I think if people knew more about the resources and efforts that go into producing the food on their table, they'd never waste a morsel.

We must honor Mother Earth by treasuring her resources.

Everything and everyone has value, including experiences. Always keep the value from your experiences, especially what you learn from the negative ones, so that you may never repeat them.

When I say *value,* I mean anything that enhances your life, or serves your growth. It could be knowledge that you gained from an experience, or an inspirational memory of something you cherish. If it was a negative situation, or an interaction with people you'd prefer to forget, even if you cannot see any value in it, you can make a determination to never behave like the unpleasant people you encountered. That's valuable in itself.

The right to use my professional name, Tina Turner, was the value I kept from my first marriage, when I'd left everything else behind.

Earth provides enough to satisfy everyone's need,
but not enough for everyone's greed.
—MAHATMA GANDHI

•

Peace is inextricably linked with
our love and respect for Mother Earth.
—CORETTA SCOTT KING

•

Humankind did not weave the web of life.
We are but one strand in it.
Whatever we do to the web, we do to ourselves.
All things are bound together. All things connect.
—CHIEF SEATTLE

After spending two years in legal battles, haggling with my ex about who would get what in the divorce, I was jolted by a flash of wisdom. While I was chanting, my inner voice said: *Let go of everything connected to him. Let go of the past. Let him have it all. Wipe the slate clean and start over.*

So, I told the judge that I was changing my divorce petition. I wanted nothing—only my stage name; I had worked too hard to lose that value. And I got it.

That's not to say that I ever confused my personal identity with my professional persona. I understand that I am not my profession, and this clarity has kept me grounded, centered, and sane.

Anna Mae puts on the magical cloak of Tina Turner to share entertainment and inspiration with the world. I honor and respect the public me *and* the person I am at home. But at the end of the day, I understand that my truest identity is my greater self, the part of me that infuses my life with compassion and a desire to spread hope to others.

I believe that a healthy understanding of the difference between our roles in the world and our true self is important for all of us. Everyone takes on different roles at different times, depending on our circumstances. But I hope you'll remember that there is always more to you than any one role could define.

Keeping my professional persona as Tina Turner was a triumph for me, even if it didn't pay off right away. On the material level I had almost nothing—two cars and mountains of debt—yet, on the spiritual level, I felt I had the world.

I had my independence. To me, that was everything.

There were times when I cried my heart out while I chanted away, praying for my future, yet appreciating just being alive. I began loving myself and my life, even with nothing else (yet) to show for it. Little Anna Mae finally found herself, and it was the sweetest of homecomings. What could be more valuable than that?

Now, that's not to say everything was coming up roses. Although I felt joy and freedom like never before, creating the life I wanted was a lot of hard work. Standing up against the winds of lawsuits, debts, family dramas, and chasing seemingly unreachable career goals, I matched the crash of impossibility's thunder with my roar of chanting Nam-myoho-renge-kyo.

In this intense spiritual battle, I called up my deepest inner wisdom, and suddenly, one day, the fight within was over. I let go of all doubts and any thoughts of limitation. I let go of what my lesser self told me was possible or impossible.

I had won the most important struggle of all. For the first time in my life, I saw myself with crystal clarity. What a sweet relief and freedom that was. Even though I didn't like a lot of the things I saw, I knew I could change them, which was a hopeful, empowering realization. I was now the writer, director, and producer of my life.

Although nothing in my environment had changed much, at least not on the surface, once my internal spiritual battles had been won, I knew it was only a matter of time before the changes within would be reflected in my outer world.

I also realized that I must be willing to leave my comfort zone before I could truly fly, just as birds must let go of the branch before they can soar into the sky.

I spent a long time enduring difficulties until I could transform them into realized dreams, longer than I would have liked or imagined. But I'm glad that I never gave up and kept reaching for what I wanted, both for myself and for what I could do for others. It made the victories even more meaningful. Looking back on my life, I see that it took longer for me to grow in some ways because I was handicapped by a tumultuous childhood. I was definitely what you would call a late bloomer.

After my stroke, as I read up on brain function and development, I learned that when a person is raised in an environment of chronic instability and dysfunction, the synapses in the brain don't form optimally. Perhaps that is one of the disadvantages I had from the start, and one of the reasons for my late maturity.

Whatever might have been the cause of a disadvantage in life, the only thing that really matters is what we do about it, and how we live from that moment forward.

Whatever stage of life you're in right now, always move forward, rolling like a mighty river, ever forward.

Now that my river has passed the age of eighty, within my heart I feel more youthful than ever. My spiritual practice galvanizes me to live each day with awareness of the present moment and reminds me to keep my eye on the future. With all my health challenges, every day feels like an extra blessing and more sweet icing on the cake of my life.

I like to remind myself that growing old and aging are not necessarily the same thing. As German-Swiss author Hermann Hesse said, the more we mature, the younger we grow. What a beautiful sentiment!

No matter your age, as you continue to mature, I hope you will always grow younger and keep moving forward.

If you come to an impasse and are uncertain of how to move forward, find an area of life where you can take a step to improve and advance, even if only a baby step.

Don't wait until you think you are good enough at doing something new before you venture into uncharted territory. If we all waited until we thought we had enough talent to tackle a new challenge, nothing would ever get accomplished.

My sons loved the water when they were young, so I hired a swim coach for them. But imagine if they refused to get in a pool until they learned how to swim first. They'd have waited a very long time and would have never become great swimmers.

The way you learn to swim is by plunging into the water and going through the motions with someone who can show you how to stay afloat and eventually glide around with ease.

If there's any forward movement that you've been putting off because you think you aren't good enough to start, go ahead, jump in!

Change your life today.
Don't gamble on the future,
act now, without delay.
—SIMONE DE BEAUVOIR

•

Whatever you can do or dream you can, begin it.
Boldness has genius, power and magic in it.
—JOHN ANSTER

•

It is good to have an end to journey towards,
but it is the journey that matters in the end.
—URSULA K. LE GUIN

Everyone accomplishes their human revolution in their own time. My biggest transformations came later in life. Personal progress is not a race, so take your time and go at your own pace.

Always remember that your history is not your identity. We have a chance to re-create ourselves and start anew every day.

My success as a solo artist came after many recalibrations and hard-won victories—nothing was easy—and took a long time. But when the breakthrough came, it was seismic. Suddenly, seemingly overnight, Tina Turner was everywhere. On the radio, on MTV, on talk shows, in *Mad Max Beyond Thunderdome,* at concert stadiums, in magazines, and in the background music at your dentist's office.

Like volcanic eruptions, my breakthroughs resulted from a tremendous amount of energy, built up over long periods, from activities that were mostly private, like my late-night work preparations, chanting, reading, and moments of honest self-reflection. All the while, I held this saying from Nichiren close to my heart: "Where there is unseen virtue, there will be visible reward."

The greatest visible reward of my work behind the scenes was that I was able to perform live for tens of millions of people during my career.

This achievement was something I prayed for and visualized over and over. I wanted to touch the hearts of as many people as possible with my music and performances.

I also visualized winning multiple Grammy Awards, which came true when I won for my album *Private Dancer*.

I get teary-eyed thinking about it now. I also get emotional when I recall the days so long ago in my thirties and forties when I visualized my future husband and our home together. As I sat together with Erwin this very morning at breakfast, I had a déjà vu moment and realized that our love and our home are exactly what I'd dreamed of so long ago.

Our home on Lake Zürich is not far from pastures that remind me of Nutbush, which is yet another reason why I've always liked Switzerland. It's hard to describe in words, but somehow Mother Nature cradles me here with a love that comes from both outside me and within me. That nurturing feeling of love was the theme of the 2014 Beyond album, *Love Within*.

I was the daughter of a woman who didn't want me. Her rejection led me later in life to seek love in unhealthy places, a fruitless search that kept my self-image and life condition so low that I attracted and tolerated insane levels of abuse.

The healing that my spiritual practice afforded me is what I shared in my message for *Love Within*. Whether or not we received the nurturing love of a mother, or any parental figure, as adults we can now become that nourishing source of love for ourselves.

Finding this "motherly love" within has tremendous healing power and aids our ability to forgive both ourselves and others. Developing my self-love and revealing the light of my Buddha nature has been the key to embracing my life's journey, including all my flaws and imperfections. That's how I found my true self.

In finding myself, I discovered that I am a key holder, as are you.

You are just as capable of loving yourself and accessing your Buddha nature as I am. Whether consciously aware of it or not, we all hold this key within us to unlock the gates of our own salvation and open the doors to our dreams.

This beacon of "Buddhaful" light within our hearts and minds can attract everything we need for our lasting happiness; we must simply reveal it. When we do, we realize that every change we desire outside ourselves first begins with a change within ourselves.

Coming home to our true self can take time, but like the old saying, patience is a virtue. I must say, if there's one virtue I have an abundance of, it's patience. I'm grateful for it and I know it comes from my spiritual practice.

In Buddhist scriptures, another name for a Buddha is "one who can endure." Whenever you endure challenges, remember with pride that you are demonstrating a noble characteristic of Buddhahood.

There's an expression—"Hurt people hurt people." If you have been hurt, then you must heal yourself before you hurt anyone else (or yourself). I have no doubt that Ike was one of these "hurt people," but it took me a long time after my divorce to feel compassion for him.

Challenges make you discover things about yourself
that you never knew. They're what
make the instrument stretch,
what make you go beyond the norm.
—CICELY TYSON

•

You are not judged by the height you have risen,
but from the depth you have climbed.
—FREDERICK DOUGLASS

•

It's one of the greatest gifts
you can give yourself, to forgive.
—MAYA ANGELOU

Eventually, I came to terms with the fact that Ike must have been suffering a living hell within himself to treat me and our children the way he did.

Thanks to my many years of chanting and healing, I found myself able to forgive him.

I have seldom spoken publicly about forgiveness. Sometimes, people get the wrong idea when I say that I have forgiven the people in my life who caused me pain. Forgiving people for the wrongs they've committed isn't the same as excusing or condoning their negative actions. The law of cause and effect is strict, and no one can escape the effects of their actions, forgiven or not.

I've taken to heart the importance of forgiveness and self-reflection rather than blame. Mostly, I've done so for my own sake, because I realized that the only person harmed by holding on to pain from the past is me.

In society, too, as we stand up against wrongdoing and injustices, we must keep peace, love, and forgiveness in our hearts so that our spiritual powers will grow. It is only by breaking the cycles of negativity that we can help ourselves, and others, to rise.

Feeling resentful and angry, wanting revenge for what others have done, holding on to any part of the negative experiences we've gone through at the hands of others—these are the heavy chains with which negativity binds itself to us.

Why would anyone want that?

The freeing mind-set of forgiveness and self-reflection

can be applied to every experience in our daily lives, not only to the big stuff. Whenever we feel irritated, upset, or annoyed, we should remember the sediment within us (as we saw in chapter four) and ask ourselves if we want to increase our sediment and irritation, or decrease it. If the answer is decrease—as I hope it always is—then the next step is to view whatever happened as an opportunity to build our wisdom and compassion, let go of negativity, and purify our karma.

After I started seeing upsetting situations as an opportunity for transformation, the karmic patterns that previously plagued me faded away. I had learned the universal lesson that holding on to blaming others only prolongs the pain and invites it back again.

Taking responsibility for any ways I may have contributed to a negative experience, I let it go, and free myself from it forever. This is how I healed the wounds in my heart, with tenacious compassion for myself and others.

By healing ourselves, we can also help our children, and our children's children, to be whole as they start their own journeys through life. Over the past ten years, I've had the pleasure of working with children from diverse backgrounds, sharing with them the message that they have a powerful inner world that can affect their outer world.

In these youth workshops, I explain what I wish I had been taught as a child—that we all have positive and negative life conditions within us, and it's up to us to make decisions and take actions that elevate our positive side so we can become happy. The essence of these children's workshops is captured in the album *Children Beyond,* which has received a heartening response from families around the world who use this album to introduce the topics of interfaith respect and unity to their children.

When I think of children, my mind fills with images of my beloved sons. I lost my son Craig in the summer of 2018, while I was in Paris with Erwin to celebrate our anniversary and attend our friend Giorgio Armani's fashion show. After the show, I was exhausted and about to go to bed when Erwin received an urgent message from Los Angeles.

We learned that Craig had died by suicide.

It's been almost two years now as I write this, but I miss Craig as much as ever. My youngest son, Ronnie, and I know more than anyone that Craig suffered from profound loneliness, which I believe was related to clinical depression. He had wonderful friends and was close to his younger brother and sister-in-law, but he suffered in silence. It wasn't until his sudden death that I began to understand that Craig faced serious mental health challenges, ones he was not equipped to overcome on his own.

Sadly, there still remains a stigma about mental health issues that often prevents people from seeking help. This seems to be particularly true for men, and I think it's even worse for Black men, like my son. For much of Craig's adult life, he used alcohol to deal with his problems, which only exacerbated matters, and we're sure that alcohol factored into his death.

In late July 2018, we celebrated Craig's life with two beautiful memorials, one for relatives and closest friends, and another that was open to the public. Both were wonderful tributes to all the goodness he shared with the world, highlighting his kindness, humor, sincerity, and many talents (he was an amazing chef, for one). Craig will be forever missed.

One of the messages we shared in Craig's memory, a message I want to impress upon you now, is this:

If you, or anyone you know, suffers from mental health issues, please reach out for help.

Mental health issues are the same as physical health issues—both require attention and treatment. If you have a physical ailment, such as a broken arm, a fever that won't end, diabetes, or any other health problem, you go to a doctor. You wouldn't suffer in silence and try to deal with it alone. Mental health issues are just as serious, if not more so, and require professional help.

I'm not sure if Craig's loneliness and related problems were worsened by influences like social media and phone addiction. But since his death in 2018, I can't help noticing news stories about an epidemic of loneliness, particularly among young people. Teenagers and twentysomethings are now reportedly the loneliest generations, experiencing levels of loneliness that surpass even the oldest generations (like mine), which typically report very high levels of acute loneliness. It's a mental health crisis.

We can cure physical diseases with medicine,
but the only cure for loneliness, despair,
and hopelessness is love.
—MOTHER TERESA

The worst loneliness is
not to be comfortable with yourself.
—MARK TWAIN

You have to know that your real home is within.
—QUINCY JONES

This crisis doesn't surprise me. Everywhere I go I see people staring into their smartphones and ignoring, or being oblivious to, the people around them. Somewhere along the way, the word *friend* lost its real meaning and has come to include people you barely know, and interact with only online.

It seems to me that, although social media might have started as a truly social activity at its inception, it has largely turned into "antisocial media." The youngest generations are clearly suffering the most from this new reality. I'm afraid this is a symptom of our technological evolution surpassing the rate of our spiritual evolution.

When I finished the sixth grade, less than 10 percent of households in the United States had a television. My only exposure to mass media was the radio, or an occasional film at the movie theater. Now, billions of people have television, movies, and virtually limitless amounts of other information (and disinformation) at their fingertips. This worries me.

Don't get me wrong. I like reading the comments on my online accounts as much as anyone. But I also know there is a lot of toxicity online, and many people aren't as kind to others in the virtual world as my fans are to me.

Commonplace distortions in the online world—with manipulated images and selective sharing that shows people enjoying a seemingly carefree, "perfect" life—are an unhealthy influence on the mind, especially young minds. From the priorities I see being valued online today, and in the media in general, it's no wonder that many people think that aspiring to be a billionaire is the most important thing in the world. It's no wonder people feel increasingly divided and lonely.

In reality, what we need most right now are legions of billionaires of the heart, multitudes of masters of the mind, and models of peace, equality, and unity in diversity. That, in my opinion, is what upcoming generations need to see.

I hope that, somehow, in the near future, the various technological poisons that society is facing can be turned into healing medicine.

At the moment, the best solution is to simply spend less time on our phones, tablets, and computers and more time with each other, with real human beings, face-to-face, heart-to-heart.

When I'm at home with Erwin, we make it a point not to get distracted by phones at mealtimes. Not that screens and devices are the only culprits. I often find it hard to tear myself away from the book I'm reading—I know you can relate if you love to read as much as I do. But I resist, because no novel can compare to sharing time with my dear partner.

I know that the last thing anyone ever wants to do is think about death, but as someone who has faced my own mortality time and again, I am all too aware that life is short and can end at any moment. Being always aware of the limited time we have here on Earth, and making the most of it, for the good of all, is also a part of my spiritual practice.

Do I want to spend whatever precious time I may have left—or whatever time my loved ones may have left—glued to an electronic screen? Once that time is gone, it's gone forever, and I don't want to have squandered it.

So if you're having a hard time imagining untethering yourself from your screens to have face-to-face interactions with the people in your life, think about the fact that you can never know how long you, or the people you love, will be around. It'll help you break that habit, I promise you.

Weaning ourselves off screens not only gives us more time for heart-to-heart interactions with our loved ones, it also opens up opportunities to speak with strangers on the street, or in the coffee shop, and make new friends. It's important to get out of our bubbles and meet people from different backgrounds, to open each other's minds and prevent the siloing of people into echo chambers that reflect only their own opinions.

We must do our part to prevent barriers from rising between one human heart and another. We must curb the trend of neighbors no longer knowing each other, while they seek a sense of shared identity with people elsewhere, perhaps even in other countries, separating themselves along racial, religious, or national lines. This fracturing of society is unsustainable.

We all have a number of aspects to our identities. My identity has included many ingredients in this lifetime, including: daughter, sister, Baptist, singer, American, mother, Buddhist, actress, Swiss, spouse, and more. But the most important, core identity that I share with you and every other person on the planet is this: human.

I believe that only by awakening to this shared identity can we save ourselves, individually and collectively, from the problems we face around the world. We must urgently work together to find solutions that can transform the global poisons of systemic racism and homophobia, climate crisis, pandemics, loss of the Amazon jungle, factory farming of animals, fossil fuel consumption, nuclear weapons, plastic pollution, and more.

The universal solution to all of the problems confronting humanity is for us to unite as one global team, honoring our truest roots as members of the same circle of life.

Uniting in this spirit is my hope and prayer for future generations.

These thoughts were on my mind as a rainbow of humanity welcomed me and Erwin to the Big Apple with open arms on November 7, 2019. We had come to town for the opening night of *Tina: The Tina Turner Musical,* and as we made our way through the bustling streets of New York City, I was thrilled to reach the Lunt-Fontanne Theatre and see the bright gold signage bearing my name.

The Broadway gala celebrating my musical that night was emotional and joyous, and I appreciated every minute of it. All of our guests had a great time, and I felt so proud.

Back home in Zürich the following week, Erwin and I enjoyed a quiet moment in the garden, watching the late-autumn sky as it quickly turned into a crimson sunset.

You really can change the world if you care enough.
—MARIAN WRIGHT EDELMAN

•

Just don't give up trying to do
what you really want to do.
Where there is love and inspiration,
I don't think you can go wrong.
—ELLA FITZGERALD

•

You are your best thing.
—TONI MORRISON

Erwin and I paused before going back inside the house, listening to a gorgeous birdsong in the distance. As the sound faded, we made our way into the kitchen, where we prepared a lovely dinner. We talked about my upcoming birthday, the number eight, and the age of eighty, which are meaningful in spiritual lore.

Book lover that I am, I'd been researching these subjects and found all types of interesting information.

Nichiren said that Shakyamuni Buddha summed up the entire Lotus Sutra in eight characters, which translates as "You should rise and greet them from afar, showing them the same respect you would a Buddha." This indicates that the spirit of the Lotus Sutra, and by extension Nam-myoho-renge-kyo, is to show deep respect to all living beings.

Many Asian cultures regard the number eight as auspicious, representing good fortune, opening, and growing. This is because the character for eight, when written in traditional Japanese and Chinese script, looks like a widening path, or opening door, which is seen as a sign of good fortune.

It is said that when Shakyamuni was eighty, he persuaded the leaders of a large and powerful kingdom bent on conquering their neighbors to put down their weapons and live in peaceful coexistence.

Moses was also said to have been eighty when he initially spoke to the pharaoh on behalf of his people.

And the lotus flower, the universal symbol of Buddhism, has eight petals, which is why the number eight reminds me of it. So when I visualized the age of eighty, I saw ten eight-petaled lotus flowers of varying colors swirling in the sky, like a vibrant scene from a Bollywood film.

When I talk about the significance of becoming an octogenarian, it sometimes prompts people to ask, "If you could go back in time and change something in your eighty years of life, what would you change?"

My answer? Nothing.

The good, the bad, the ugly, and the pretty, it all adds up to me. I honor my journey, all of it. Changing the past would mean changing me. And I like me, just the way I am. Why would I want to change anything?

Depending on who asks the question, I occasionally throw a curveball with a deeper, more philosophical answer, along these lines:

I've already changed my past, by turning poison into medicine, and by raising my life condition, which transforms my perception of the past. Our perception determines the way events affect us. So, when we change the way a past event affects us, we effectively change the past.

In other words, since past, present, and future are seamlessly connected, a change in the present moment has the power to affect a change in everything throughout all directions of space and time.

Every now and then, when I share this answer, I'm told that I sound like a Jedi master from *Star Wars,* so I don't share it often. But I hope you enjoy hearing it.

On an even deeper level, the reason I happily and gratefully accept everything I went through in the past is because I believe every detail of my life is both my karma and my mission.

We are all born with a mission, a purpose, that only we can fulfill.

When you live with a joyful sense of purpose, when you infuse your life with a greater purpose beyond your individual self, every aspect of your karma can become a brilliant facet of your mission. You can transform sorrow and adversity of any sort into joy, stability, health, and prosperity. By changing poison into medicine and accomplishing your inner revolution, you can use every experience of karma to encourage others who suffer from the same problems that you overcame.

You can become an ambassador of hope, an essential and radiant treasure of humanity, in which you recognize that all who have ever lived are members of your extended family.

As you continue to spread light in this way, actively doing good in the world, that energy will come back to you in abundant positivity. When you refuse to perpetuate any bad that has been done to you, you can free yourself from the chains of negativity.

Use your life for peace and goodwill.

Keep on going until you climb the summit of your happiest dreams.

I hope that what I've offered in this little book will be of service to you in your ascent to new heights of fulfillment.

Thank you for letting me share my life with you. Thank you for opening your heart and mind to my words.

I wish you well on your journey to joy, and I leave you with this final thought, my greatest wish and prayer for you:

please
never give up,

keep on
making the impossible possible,

turning
poison into medicine,

so you
may become truly happy,

because
happiness becomes you,

forever.

AFTERWORD

By Taro Gold and Regula Curti

TARO GOLD: The force of nature that is Tina Turner first appeared to me on New Year's Eve 1981. I had just turned twelve and was on holiday break from my job performing with the first national touring company of the Broadway musical *Evita*.

I don't recall anything about that night before I turned on the TV. What I do recall is this: As the TV screen came on, a woman I didn't recognize was singing and dancing, lighting up a concert stage in a whirlwind of sheer magnetic energy.

Who in the world is she? I wondered.

I called for my mom to come and see—maybe she would recognize this mystery woman, since they seemed about the same age.

"I haven't seen her in years," Mom said, "but I'm pretty sure that's Tina. She looks great!"

"Tina who?" I asked.

"Tina Turner."

And just like that, as soon as I heard her name, Tina finished the set and was gone. It was a powerful first impression that left her timeless energy etched in my psyche.

I don't recall seeing Tina again until her song "What's Love Got to Do with It" took the planet by storm in 1984. Soon, her joyful presence was all around the media, and my mom often filled our home with the sound of Tina's masterpiece album *Private Dancer*.

REGULA CURTI: My first experience with Tina Turner was in 1983. I was twenty-seven and facing a difficult time in my life.

I'd grown up in a cosmopolitan Swiss family, embedded in a conservative society. And yet it was also a time of women's emancipation. Torn between being an obedient daughter who wanted to please others and my wild, rebellious side, I worried I'd never find my true potential.

Having joined the Swiss Armed Forces at twenty, where women had equal rights and duties, I glimpsed a wider view of modern womanhood. Yet living with my first husband in a small Swiss village tucked into a narrow valley, my fear—both physical and emotional—of being buried alive increased.

That all changed one cold December night at the Zürich Convention Center, where I witnessed Tina electrify the stage, wildly dancing in a shiny red dress, like a glamorous thunderbolt.

As she filled the air with her soulful voice, it seemed this woman before my eyes had no limits to her energy, her freedom, her life force. My heart instantly felt full as I watched her performance. I sensed there was more I could do, more I could dream, more I could become.

Leaving the concert that night, I let go of my sense of limitations. Never in my wildest dreams did I expect such a life-changing experience from a rock 'n' roll show—it was by far the greatest gift of inspiration I'd ever received from a performer.

Within a year, Tina achieved her global breakthrough as a solo artist. I basked in the sounds of her performances on the radio and television. Tina helped me set my life on a new trajectory, and hearing her voice always reminded me of the joy I felt that special time I'd shared space with her on my night of inner liberation.

TARO: In 1986, my father suddenly passed away. To relieve my sadness, and "turn poison into medicine," I decided to join my mother and Japanese aunties as they chanted Nam-myoho-renge-kyo together each day.

About six months after I started chanting, I heard an interview with Tina in which she talked about her practice of Buddhism. She said she dreamed of writing a book to share her spiritual journey with the world, and to encourage people to never give up on their dreams.

A light went on in the back of my mind, like a whisper

of awareness saying to me, *You're going to help her do that someday.*

At the time, I was a sixteen-year-old beach boy in Southern California, and I wasn't sure what the message meant. But my heart told me to remember it—*remember the future.*

REGULA: By the time the Berlin Wall fell in 1989, I had built up my confidence and independent spirit. My inner voice was getting stronger, telling me to be confident and true to myself.

I'd been married for nearly a decade, but deep down I knew it wasn't the right relationship for my happiness. One night, I dreamed of a large, mirrorlike lake with stunning white flowers on the far shore. I jumped in and swam toward the flowers. It felt like a leap toward my future, my truth, my joy.

Recalling the inspiration I felt from Tina's example, I decided to divorce.

Four years later, I met the love of my life, Beat Curti, whom I soon married.

TARO: After I graduated from university in 1994, I moved to West Los Angeles, where I met Ana and Wayne Shorter at a neighborhood chanting meeting. Ana had overcome severe difficulties through her Buddhist practice, including serious addiction problems, and she shared profound life lessons with me. Wayne was a mix of musical master, Bodhisattva,

Santa Claus, and wise spiritual uncle whose unique voice I could listen to all day long.

A couple years later, I met Tina's son Craig. He loved that my first name was Craig, too, which everybody called me until my teen years, when I decided to go by my middle name, Taro.

Craig was always very thoughtful and kind, and he was a brilliant chef—he made some excellent vegan meals for me. I also heard wonderful things about his mother from him, as well as from Ana and Wayne.

They told me that Tina always encouraged people around her, her employees on tour, drivers, hotel staff. Anyone she came in contact with, Tina would ask about their lives and offer them warm advice.

Sometimes people asked her to teach them about chanting, and she'd always send them to Ana and Wayne's place. There, I became close with a number of such people over the years, each of whom told me their own stories about Tina's deep sense of caring and natural wisdom.

During Tina's Wildest Dreams tour in the late 1990s, I was privileged to receive backstage passes in Europe, Australia, and the United States. The faces of the audiences I saw on that tour were unforgettable. No matter where we went, no matter what age, race, or gender of the people, I saw everyone shed tears when Tina appeared onstage.

At first, I thought it must just be the front rows, since they were very close to her. So I went to the backs of the stadiums and found it was the same. I even teared up myself. I'd been to many different concerts by various artists over the years, but never saw anything like it before.

Everyone shed tears when they saw Tina. But why?

REGULA: One day in 2001, a friend asked my husband, Beat, to meet with someone who was curious about one of Beat's prior homes. It seemed the new occupant wanted to know who'd lived there before, what type of events or parties had taken place, and what previous residents thought about the energy of the property.

The home was called Château Algonquin, and to our surprise, the new people living there were Tina Turner and her partner, Erwin Bach.

Out of the blue, my personal heroine invited us to dine with her! I was thrilled.

At dinner, we were welcomed to a gorgeous round table that Tina had decorated with a magnificent candelabra centerpiece, decorative objects, and white flowers. Tina and I bonded over spiritual discussions, and I felt like we had known each other forever.

It was like a dream come true, only I hadn't even dreamed it. Or had I?

Turns out the property is on a large, mirrorlike lake (Lake Zürich), and there in front of me was an array of beautiful white flowers—the same things I'd seen in my dream ten years earlier.

TARO: I told my friends who worked and toured with Tina about my observations—that everyone in the audience cried when Tina appeared onstage. It was mystical and magical, and very real.

They said they knew the answer: Tina chanted for an hour before every show, praying for the true happiness of each audience member. She prayed she could provide whatever each person needed to ignite hope in their heart.

That's what I saw in all those faces around the world— Tina's wish for people's happiness was so strong and pure, it moved whole stadiums to tears.

REGULA: I shed tears when I think of Tina's compassion. And in 2009, I shed tears of joy when I found myself dancing for Tina at her seventieth birthday party.

That year, we had musically collaborated for the first time with Beyond Music, and as her seventieth birthday approached, Tina asked me to be one of her backup singers and dancers for some private birthday fun.

In her garage, three times per week for several weeks, Tina taught me and five other girlfriends her dance routines for "Proud Mary," "Steamy Windows," and "Simply the Best." She was determined to bring out in each of us our greatest potential, our hidden personality traits, strengths, and beauty.

She gave us meticulous advice on our movements, expressions, shoes, fashion, hair, and makeup. She had an eagle eye for details. The result was a golden memory of reveling in her seventieth birthday festivities with her. Having Tina as my mentor in performing meant everything to me.

That experience transformed my life, and I became a better performer because of her caring instruction. From that point on, I felt freer and more confident onstage.

Tina showed me that I have wings—we all do.

TARO: In the 2000s, I wrote a series of bestselling books based on Eastern wisdom and things I'd learned living and studying in Japan as a teenager and university student. I enjoyed traveling around the United States and the world, doing book signings.

From the time I met my husband, Wendell, in 1995 and throughout the 2000s, we also enjoyed exploring the globe together. Starting in 2005, we visited Switzerland at least once a year.

Through a happy case of serendipity, I met Regula there in 2014.

Over tea, we shared our love of Buddhist chanting with each other and discovered the mystical intersections of Tina's life with each of ours.

REGULA: The day that Taro and I first met, I mentioned to him that Tina used to tell me of her long-held dream to write an inspirational book about her spiritual journey. But she felt the timing hadn't been quite right, plus she wanted to find a coauthor who shared her practice of Buddhism.

I'd read some books that Taro had written, and as we spoke that day over tea, I realized he shared the same Buddhist practice as Tina. I immediately suggested that he and I together could help Tina create the book she'd dreamed about writing.

Taro and I put together a book outline that we shared with Tina and Erwin. However, Tina's health challenges during that time were increasingly complex. Although everyone loved the book plan, we agreed it had to wait until Tina recovered.

TARO: *Remember the future . . .* That feeling I had at sixteen was finally made clear to me. Life had found a way to harmonize everything. As Regula once said to me, "The great organizing force of the universe has guided all our paths together."

REGULA: It was a blessing that Tina overcame her health challenges, and the labor of love to create this book began in spring 2019. Tina told me that sharing her spiritual story with the world is her ultimate gift.

TARO AND REGULA: We took that as our mandate to illuminate *Happiness Becomes You* with the legacy of Tina's heart. And by assisting Tina to express her inner explorations, our hearts gained more than we could have imagined.

Tina's wisdom inspires us to be kinder to ourselves and

others, go deeper within for answers, and become more joyful today than yesterday. Her eternal seeking spirit boosts our vision of what's possible.

Tina lights the way for us to always "polish life's mirror" so we can see ourselves clearly—and change anything for the better.

We hope you feel the same.

TARO GOLD AND REGULA CURTI
August 8, 2020

Acknowledgments

FROM TINA: I would sincerely like to give thanks to my coauthors, Regula Curti and Taro Gold, for their dedicated and graceful efforts in helping me share my thoughts.

FROM TINA, REGULA, AND TARO: We wish to express profound appreciation for our husbands, Erwin, Beat, and Wendell, respectively, for their invaluable support in creating this book.

We also offer our gratitude to Anna Wichmann, to the Looping Group, to Richard Pine, and to Peter Borland for their literary excellence; to Dr. Neil deGrasse Tyson and to Dr. Andrew Barron for their keen scientific reviews and insights; and to the many others behind the scenes who helped make this book shine.

GLOSSARY

Alaya

The eighth consciousness level of the mind, a storehouse in which reside the results of all our thoughts, words, and deeds; all of our personal memories, conscious or otherwise; as well as the collective memory of all humankind. Also called *alaya* consciousness or storehouse consciousness. (*See also:* nine consciousnesses.)

Amala

The ninth consciousness level of the mind, the shining level of our Buddha nature, our greater self or pure life force, which cannot be stained by karmic accumulations and which brings forth a feeling of transcendence. Also called *amala* consciousness or pure consciousness. (*See also:* nine consciousnesses.)

Ashram

A place of religious retreat, especially in South Asia.

Bodhi tree
A large tree of the fig variety, also known as the "tree of knowledge" or "tree of awakening," because the Buddha's enlightenment is said to have occurred while he sat beneath a bodhi tree.

Bodhisattva(s)
Bodhisattvas are people who aspire to enlightenment (Buddhahood), and their predominant characteristic is considered to be compassion because they carry out altruistic practices for the sake of others. In the ancient Sanskrit language, *bodhi* means "enlightenment" and *sattva* means "essence" or "living being."

Buddha
Buddha means "Enlightened One," indicating a person who correctly perceives the true nature and impermanence of all phenomena, and who also leads others to enlightenment. The Buddha nature, which is an indestructible life force, exists in all beings and has the qualities of wisdom, courage, and compassion.

Buddha, Shakyamuni
The historical Buddha, also known as Siddhartha Gautama, or Gautama Buddha, who lived approximately 2,500 years ago between 560 B.C.E. and 480 B.C.E.; the founder of Buddhism, whose teachings are contained in collections of writings known as sutras, including the Lotus Sutra, widely considered to be his ultimate teaching. Shakyamuni means "sage of the Shakya clan."

Buddha nature, or greater self
Buddhism holds that all people possess an innate Buddha nature, which is the inherent potential for the attainment of enlightenment. Buddha nature is also the state of being and manifest life condition of a Buddha.

Buddhism

Buddhism refers to a spectrum of spiritual traditions based on the original teachings of Shakyamuni Buddha, who lived some 2,500 years ago. Buddhism is the world's fourth-largest religion, whose practitioners, known as Buddhists, compose approximately 10 percent of the global population.

Buddhism, Nichiren

A school of Buddhism that originated with the teachings of Nichiren (1222–1282), a religious reformer and philosopher in thirteenth-century Japan. Nichiren taught that the title, or *daimoku,* of the Lotus Sutra (Nam-myoho-renge-kyo) contains the essence of Buddhist teachings.

Butsudan

Japanese for "Buddhist altar," a butsudan is a shrine or altar that holds the Gohonzon, or mandala, commonly found in SGI Buddhist centers and in the homes of those who practice Buddhism.

Cause and effect

The Buddhist principle that all actions (thoughts, words, and deeds) have consequences, positive or negative, depending on the quality and intention of the action. Consequences are considered to be neither reward nor punishment, merely consequential results. Buddhism expounds that the law of cause and effect is universal, operating throughout all life and spanning past, present, and future existences. The law of cause and effect (also called the Mystic Law of cause and effect, or causality) is the foundation of the doctrine of karma.

Chakras

The Sanskrit word *chakra* means "wheel," and in ancient Eastern medicinal traditions indicates key energy points and the movement of energy within one's body. The *dharma-chakra,* or the wheel of the Law, is often used to describe the teachings of Buddhism, as it indicates turning of the wheels of enlightenment.

Chanting
Chanting is a spiritual discipline of active meditation and prayer, typically with the repeated vocalization or singing of a mantra such as Nam-myoho-renge-kyo.

Daimoku
Japanese for "title," *daimoku* refers to Nam-myoho-renge-kyo, the title of the Lotus Sutra.

Dependent origination
"No man is an island," as poet John Donne writes. Dependent origination is a Buddhist doctrine expressing the interdependence of all things, and that no beings or phenomena exist on their own; they exist or occur because of their relationship with other beings and causes and conditions. That is, nothing can exist independent of other things or arise in isolation. By recognizing our innate connection to all beings and situations, we are motivated to feel compassion for others. Also called dependent causation or conditioned co-arising.

Ego
The ego is a feeling of separateness, a sense of duality, or a notion of being different or superior to others. It is the false perception of oneself as a separate being apart from the greater web of life or from others and often leads to a sense of self-importance, arrogance, or anger.

Enlightenment

The attainment of Buddhahood in one's present form as an ordinary person. The Lotus Sutra teaches that there is no need to transform any characteristics of oneself to become an enlightened person.

Four noble truths

A fundamental doctrine of Buddhism that clarifies the true cause of suffering and the way of emancipation, or total freedom. The four noble truths are: (1) the truth of suffering, that all existence is suffering; (2) the truth of the origin of suffering, which is selfish craving; (3) the truth of the cessation of suffering, the eradication of selfish craving that enables one to attain a state of total happiness; (4) the truth of the path to the cessation of suffering.

Gohonzon

The scroll image used as the point of focus while chanting the mantra (Nam-myoho-renge-kyo) of the Soka Gakkai Buddhist tradition. As the physical embodiment of Nam-myoho-renge-kyo, the Gohonzon expresses the enlightened aspects of the Ten Worlds, especially Buddhahood, which all people inherently possess. In Japanese, *Go* is an honorary prefix that indicates "worthy of respect," and *honzon* indicates "fundamental object." Nichiren described the Gohonzon as the "fundamental object [mandala] for observing one's mind."

Gongyo

In Japanese, literally, to "exert [oneself in] practice." *Gongyo* refers to the twice-daily Soka Gakkai Buddhist practice of reciting portions of the second and sixteenth chapters of the Lotus Sutra, plus chanting Nam-myoho-renge-kyo.

Greater self

The greater self is a broad sense of self that can fully identify and empathize with the suffering of others, grounded in wisdom and respect for the dignity of all life and its interdependence. One who challenges self-centeredness with altruistic action greatly expands the lesser self toward the ideal of the greater self.

Human revolution

The process of positive transformation of one's character; breaking through the shackles of the ego-centered "lesser self." In this process, one reveals one's "greater self," experiencing an inner transformation of deep compassion and joy in taking action for the sake of others, and ultimately, all living beings.

Karma

Karma is a Sanskrit word meaning "action." The doctrine of karma is based on the law of cause and effect and is an accumulation of our actions in thoughts, words, and deeds (causes) made in the past. These causes reside in the inner realm of life as potential energies until the circumstances arise for them to manifest as effects. Individual karma can be seen as karmic results related to the microcosm of a particular living being.

Beyond individual karma, there is also collective karma. As a family, as a neighborhood, as a society, as a nation, as humanity, as a global community of living beings, and so forth, we share in the karmic results of the wider web of life. Even if we as individuals have not directly participated in a particular action within our society or world, because we are connected to the broader group we will also experience the consequences. Collective karma can be viewed as karmic results related to the macrocosm of our entire world.

Karmic patterns

Karmic patterns are habitual or subconscious behaviors and attitudes that one feels compelled to repeat.

Lesser self

The lesser self is a narrow sense of self that cannot feel empathy or compassion. It is the ego, which can enslave us to selfish desires and cause suffering for both ourselves and others.

Lotus Sutra

The Lotus Sutra is widely considered to contain Shakyamuni Buddha's ultimate teaching. Its essence is its title, Nam-myoho-renge-kyo, the chanting and practice of which can open the door to enlightenment for all. Also called the Lotus Sutra of the Wonderful Law or the Sutra of the Lotus Blossom of the Fine Dharma, the Lotus Sutra is a Chinese translation of the Sanskrit scripture *Saddharma-pundarika-sutra,* compiled by the Buddhist scholar Kumarajiva in 406. It consists of eight volumes and twenty-eight chapters. (*See also:* Buddhism, Nichiren.)

Mandala

A spiritual object of devotion or focus and symbol of enlightenment. In Japanese traditions, mandalas are often in scroll form and depict Buddhas, Bodhisattvas, the various life conditions of living beings, and other doctrinal symbols. (*See also:* Gohonzon.)

Mantra

Mantra, in Sanskrit, means "tool" or "instrument of the mind." Mantras are typically brief repeated words or phrases either spoken, sung, or chanted (such as Nam-myoho-renge-kyo) that can be used as a form of meditation or activation of the mind and spirit.

Nine consciousnesses
Nine types of discernment and awareness. The first five consciousnesses correspond to the five senses: sight, hearing, smell, taste, and touch.

The sixth consciousness integrates and translates the perception of the five senses into coherent images and makes judgments about the external, physical world.

The seventh consciousness corresponds to one's inner world. Awareness of and attachment to the ego, or lesser self, originate from the seventh consciousness. The seventh consciousness is also the realm of imagination and determining the difference between right and wrong. (*See also:* ego *and* lesser self.)

The eighth consciousness, also known as the *alaya* consciousness, exists in the subconscious level of our mind, where all our previous thoughts, words, and deeds (karma) are stored. This eighth consciousness holds the sum of our positive and negative karma, storing it as karmic "potentials" or "seeds" that produce corresponding positive or negative consequences. (*See also: alaya.*)

The ninth consciousness, also known as the *amala,* remains free from all karmic impurity and is defined as the foundation of all life's functions. It is described as the "fundamental pure consciousness." Nichiren inscribed the Gohonzon as the embodiment of *amala* consciousness, or the ultimate reality of Buddhahood. (*See also: amala.*)

Oneness of life and its environment
A Buddhist principle that teaches that when we change ourselves, our environment simultaneously changes. It illustrates the fact that separation between oneself and one's surroundings is an illusion: Our inner life and exterior world are one and the same. The environment around us, including our work, home, family, and friends, is a reflection of our inner state. This principle reveals that life and its environment, though two seemingly distinct phe-

nomena, are essentially nondual; they are two integral phases of a single reality.

Phoenix
A symbol of positive transformation, against all odds. In classical mythology, the phoenix is a unique bird that after hundreds of years of life burns itself completely and rises again from the ashes, eternally emerging stronger, wiser, and more powerful than before.

Sangha
A community of Buddhist believers.

Shogun
In premodern Japan, the shoguns were Japan's supreme military leaders, awarded the title by the emperor. From 1603 to 1868, Japan was ruled by a series of shoguns known as the Tokugawa shogunate. The shoguns controlled foreign policy and the military and were the most important group in Japanese society, as they had greater power than any other group.

Shogunate
Shogunate indicates the system of government of a feudal military dictatorship, exercised in the name of the shogun or by the shogun himself.

Soka Gakkai International (SGI)
A community-based Buddhist network for practitioners of Nichiren Buddhism with members in 192 countries and territories. The SGI promotes cultural exchange, education, and peace through personal transformation and social contribution. In Japanese, *Soka Gakkai* means "value-creating society."

Sutra

A Sanskrit word meaning "thread," *sutra* refers to collections of Buddhist teachings or lectures.

Ten Worlds

The Lotus Sutra teaches that each of the Ten Worlds is a potential state of being or condition of life inherent in living beings. These Ten Worlds are: Hell (suffering or destructive despair), Hunger (insatiable desires), Animality (uncontrolled instinctive behaviors), Anger (ego attachments, conflict, and arrogance), Tranquility (relative calm), Heaven (temporary elation), Learning (seeking truth from the teachings or experiences of others), Realization (understanding truth through our own efforts), Bodhisattva (compassion, altruism, aspiring to enlightenment for oneself and others), and Buddhahood (total freedom, wholeness, and absolute happiness; limitless sense of unity with the life force of the universe). Each "world" contains the potential for all other worlds within it.

Three poisons

Greed, anger, and foolishness, which is sometimes referred to as ignorance or stupidity. Buddhism teaches that the three poisons are the fundamental evils inherent in life, giving rise to suffering. These poisons are the sources of all illusions and earthly desires that cause unhappiness.

Wheel of the Law

A term for the teachings of Buddhism. The preaching of a Buddha is often expressed in Buddhist scriptures as "turning the wheel of the Law." *Law* in Nichiren Buddhism refers to the Mystic Law of cause and effect, or Nam-myoho-renge-kyo.

Bibliography

Carter, Lawrence Edward, Sr. *A Baptist Preacher's Buddhist Teacher*. Santa Monica: Middleway Press, 2018.

Causton, Richard. *The Buddha in Daily Life*. London: Rider, 1995.

Derbolav, Josef, and Daisaku Ikeda. *Search for a New Humanity*. London: I.B. Tauris, 2008.

Gold, Taro. *Living Wabi Sabi: The True Beauty of Your Life*. Kansas City: Andrews McMeel Publishing, 2004.

Hancock, Herbie. *Herbie Hancock: Possibilities*. New York: Penguin, 2014.

Hawking, Stephen. *Brief Answers to the Big Questions*. New York: Bantam, 2018.

Hochswender, Woody, Greg Martin, and Ted Morino. *The Buddha in Your Mirror*. Santa Monica: Middleway Press, 2001.

Ikeda, Daisaku. *Unlocking the Mysteries of Birth & Death*. Santa Monica: Middleway Press, 2004.

Jammer, Max. *Einstein and Religion: Physics and Theology*. Princeton, NJ: Princeton University Press, 2002.

King, Martin Luther, Jr. *Why We Can't Wait*. New York: Signet Classics, 2000.

Mercer, Michelle. *Footprints: The Life & Work of Wayne Shorter*. New York: Penguin, 2007.

Ricard, Matthieu, and Trinh Xuan Thuan. *The Quantum and the Lotus*. New York: Crown, 2001.

Shorter, Wayne, Herbie Hancock, and Daisaku Ikeda. *Reaching Beyond*. Santa Monica: Middleway Press, 2018.

Turner, Tina, and Kurt Loder. *I, Tina*. New York: William Morrow, 1986.

Turner, Tina, Deborah Davis, and Dominik Wichmann. *My Love Story*. New York: Atria Books, 2018.

Tyson, Neil deGrasse, and Donald Goldsmith. *Origins*. New York: W. W. Norton, 2005.

Watson, Burton, translator. *The Lotus Sutra*. Tokyo: Soka Gakkai, 2009.

INDEX

About the Authors

TINA TURNER

Tina Turner, born Anna Mae Bullock, is a singer, dancer, and actress whose career has spanned more than sixty years. A beloved musical icon, she has sold over 200 million records and more live concert tickets than any other solo performer in history. In her private life, Tina is a deeply spiritual person whose mission is to encourage others with the lessons she has learned from many hard-won victories. For more than three decades, she has reached deep into the wellspring of her experiences to give relatives and friends personal guidance on the most effective ways to create lasting happiness in their lives. Now, in this book, she is delighted to share the story of her spiritual journey, so it can be of service to others. Having happily retired from her legendary career in entertainment, Tina resides in Switzerland with her cherished partner of thirty-four years, her husband, Erwin Bach. Her memoir *My Love Story* was an international bestseller.

tinaturnerofficial.com • Instagram: @tinaturner •
Facebook.com/tinaturner • tina-turner.rocks

TARO GOLD

Taro Gold is the author of seven bestselling inspirational books, including one of Tina's all-time favorites, *Living Wabi Sabi: The True Beauty of Your Life,* and other popular books such as *The Tao of Mom, The Tao of Dad, What Is Love?,* and *Open Your Mind, Open Your Life.* He has written extensively for Buddhist publications, including the *World Tribune* newspaper and *Living Buddhism* magazine. In his youth, Taro performed in the first U.S. national touring company of *Evita* and other Broadway musicals, including *Falsettos* and *Peter Pan.* Having spent much of his life abroad, he developed an expansive worldview, traveling to more than forty nations and living in Australia, Spain, and Japan, where he became the first American man to graduate from Soka University of Tokyo. Taro currently resides in the U.S. with his best friend of twenty-five years—his husband, Wendell Brown—and their beloved Italian greyhound, Magic.

tarogold.com · Twitter: @tarogold · Instagram: @tarogold

REGULA CURTI

Regula Curti is a multifaceted musician, music therapist, teacher, and founder of Seeschau House of Sacred Arts at Lake Zürich. She is the entrepreneurial and creative force behind Beyond Music, a global digital platform that she founded in 2007. Having earned a master's degree in expressive arts and music therapy, Regula's passion is sharing the healing and unifying power of music. Beyond Music promotes collaboration among singers and musicians from different cultures to foster peace and tolerance. Regula has produced and vocally performed on four bestselling interfaith albums that have earned gold and platinum awards, including collaborations with Tina on Beyond *Buddhist and Christian Prayers, Children* Beyond, *Love Within* Beyond, and *Awakening* Beyond. Regula resides in Switzerland with her treasured husband of nearly three decades and cofounder of the Beyond Foundation, Beat Curti.

beyond-foundation.org · Instagram: @regula.curti · Facebook.com/beyond